Best wishes

Joaquin

10/20/88.

THE
Chez François
COOKBOOK

REVISED EDITION

Jacques E. Haeringer

PRENTICE HALL PRESS · NEW YORK

pour Evelyn, Madeleine et Marc

Published by Prentice Hall Press
A Division of Simon & Schuster, Inc.
Gulf + Western Building
One Gulf + Western Plaza
New York, NY 10023

This is a revised edition of a book originally published by Reston
Publishing Company, Inc.

PRENTICE HALL PRESS is a trademark of Simon & Schuster, Inc.

Library of Congress Cataloging in Publication Data

Haeringer, Jacques.
The Chez François cookbook.

  "François Haeringer, le restaurant, c'est moi," by William Rice; p. xvii.
  Includes index.
  1. Cookery, French. 2. L'Auberge Chez François (Great Falls, Va.)
3. Haeringer, François R.
I. Title
TX719.H26   1986   641.5′09755′291   85-30070
ISBN 0-13-129693-0

Manufactured in the United States of America

10 9 8 7 6 5 4 3 2 1

First Prentice Hall Press Edition

ACKNOWLEDGMENTS

This book, like the operation of L'Auberge Chez François, took the efforts of the entire Haeringer family, members of the staff, and the assistance of many individuals.

My appreciation goes to my mother for providing the handwritten French recipe titles and rendering my fluent broken kitchen French into *bon français*; to my father for verifying the accuracy of the recipes and inspiring the hints to the home cook; to my wife Evelyn for her support, much retyping and her ferreting out and translating my *"franglais"* into *anglais*; to my brother Robert for taking on additional responsibilities at the restaurant, thereby giving me more time to write; and to my brother Paul for his fine photography.

Many thanks are due to sous chef Chun Ik Oh and pastry chef William Sobalvarro for helping me refine the recipes.

I give my sincere thanks to Rona Cohen for her aid in transcribing the bulk of the recipes and her many suggestions, and to Anne Sweda for the initial home testing and her encouraging evaluation of the recipes.

Special appreciation goes to the following enthusiastic testers and tasters who made certain my instructions could be duplicated at home: ring leader Nancy and husband Curt Loughin; Sandy and Roger Will; Trish, Jim and Beth Skaptason; Heather and Bob Greene; B.J. and Marilyn Silvey; Jo and Jerry Kirks; and Pam Jacoby.

For their encouragement and assistance, I wish to acknowledge my friends John and Constance Locke; Charles Shaw; Tom Inge; Ona McBride; the members of the Great Falls cell at the Church of the Apostles; my editors Catherine Rossbach and Ted Buchholz. *Merci beaucoup*.

CONTENTS

CONTENTS

PREFACE

I was four years old in 1954 when my father opened Chez François. French food and the restaurant business have been a part of my life for as long as I can remember. There were only three other French restaurants in the Washington area at the time. In a sense my father was a pioneer, as he was the first to offer complete meals in a less formal atmosphere. His goal then, as now, was to operate a restaurant with "a nice ambiance and good honest food at affordable prices." His continued popularity, after thirty years, is a testimony to his success with this approach.

Starting at the age of twelve, I began working summers with my father, first as a bus boy, then as a salad maker, and later as a cook. I remember my father's uncanny ability always to be on hand whenever I made a mistake. It was under his sharp eyes that I first began to learn the trade.

Not until the advanced age of twenty-two, after graduating from college, did I decide on a full-time culinary career. Before joining the business, a stint in France seemed appropriate. I arrived there in 1972 to learn *la cuisine française*. I was, without a doubt, the oldest living apprentice, as most of the cooks my age already had six or seven years' experience.

I tried to entertain the French chefs with wild west stories, and satisfy their queries about *les femmes américaines*. In exchange they patiently answered my many questions and shared their culinary experiences. Those chefs include my cousins, the Ohressers of La Charcuterie in Obernai, Alsace; Joseph Weber, owner of La Patisserie et Boulangerie Alsacienne in Paris; as well as several other restaurateurs, including Paul Haberlain, *chef patron* of the three star L'Auberge de L'Ill in Alsace.

I returned home in 1973 to discover that the Claridge Hotel, which housed Chez François, was to be sold to make room for yet another glass and concrete office building. At fifty-six, Papa decided against retirement and his thoughts turned to fulfilling his dream of opening an *auberge*, a country inn, like those in his native Alsace. A country store and antique shop on six acres of land in Great Falls was selected as the site. We smile when Papa recounts his first visit to the then Riverbend country store. He thought the realtor must be insane to suggest anyone would drive down this hilly winding lane to dine. But after rounding the top of the final hill, he saw and instantly recognized the potential of the place. This decision was made contrary to the advice of many who felt that Great Falls was too far from Washington, D.C., and that the country roads were a hindrance.

After the closing of the downtown Chez François in June, 1975, almost a year of remodeling, personally supervised by my father, was necessary before L'Auberge Chez François was completed. Much of the decor, including the front doors, the stained glass, and the large antique glass windows through which many patrons observe the kitchen was taken from the downtown restaurant. Many of the small pieces in the dining room, such as the copper bed warmers, the grandfather clocks and hand painted crockery, are Haeringer family heirlooms. The murals of Obernai, Papa's home town, were painted by artist Jerry Jerominek, an old friend, who also designed the menu cover. Even the custom-made plate and tablecoth patterns are reminiscent of those from Papa's boyhood.

Chez François
Dinner
. . . .

Suprême de Fruits --- Tomato Juice
Saumon Fumé --- Canapé D'Anchois ou Caviar --- Shrimp Cocktail 65¢ extra
Le Paté Maison --- Le Canapé de Paté de Foie
Le Potage du Jour --- La Soupe à L'Oignon Gratinée --- La Vichyssoise
Le Ramequin au Gruyère (30 minutes) 65¢ extra --- Half Grapefruit ou Canteloupe en Saison
Demi Douzaine d'Escargots 1.15 extra --- Demi Douzaine Blue Points en Saison 75¢
Harengs à la Crème

Le Filet of Sole du Jour 3.00

Les Scallops Sautés Maison 3.25
Scallops sautéd with Garlic, Shallots, Brown Butter

La Sôle Anglaise aux Amandes Grillées 3.50
English Channel Sole with Almonds

Les Escargots de Bourgogne Vigneronne 3.50
Our Snails Prepared as in France

Les Cuisses de Grenouille à la Provençale 3.50
Frog Legs with Garlic, Brown Butter

La Langouste de Chez François 3.45
Lobster Tail with Special Garlic Butter

Le Vol au Vent aux Fruits de Mer 3.40
Pattie Shell with Scallops, Lobster, Mushrooms, etc.

La Raie au Beurre Noir 3.25
Skate Fish with Capers, Brown Butter

La Coquille Saint-Jacques 3.35
Scallops in the Shell, Mushrooms, White Wine Sauce

Le Homard du Maine Grillé Françillon 3.65
Broiled Fresh Maine Lobster, Brown Butter

Ask to see our Wine List
Complete Selection for your Enjoyment

First dinner menu, 1954

xii

We opened L'Auberge Chez François April 20, 1976, with the intention of serving about seventy-five people a night. My mother was going to prepare the pastries, and my father and I together were to do all the cooking. That first night was a bit of a disaster. Papa had been unable to say no to many of his loyal customers, and L'Auberge was overbooked. Most of the staff was inexperienced, and despite the help of good

---

L'Escalope de Veau du Jour 3.25
(Scaloppini of Veal, garnished)

Le Coq au Vin à la Bourguignonne 3.25
(Chicken in Wine Sauce)

La Cervelle de Veau au Beurre Noir 3.00
(Calf's Brain with Capers, Brown Butter)

La Langue de Boeuf au Madère 3.15
(Smoked Beef Tongue, Madeira Sauce)

Le Rognon de Veau à la Forestière 3.00
(Veal Kidney, Broiled, garnished)

Rock Cornish Game Squab des Gourmets 3.50

La Côtelette de Veau Paysanne 3.35
(Veal Chop, Bacon, Onions, Mushrooms)

Le Jambon de York au Porto 3.25
(Ham in Port Wine)

Le Caneton du Long Island à L'Orange 3.35
(Long Island Duckling in Orange Sauce)

Les Côtes D'Agneau au Cresson 3.65
(Broiled Lamb Chops with Watercress)

Le Ris de Veau en Cocotte au Sherry 3.75
(Calf's Sweetbreads, Sherry Wine)

Le Foie de Veau à la Maître d'Hôtel 3.50
(Calf's Liver Sauté in Butter)

L'Entrecôte Poêlée Maison 4.00
(Steak, Minute, garnished)

Le Filet Mignon Grillé Béarnaise 4.25
(Tenderloin Steak with Béarnaise Sauce)

Le Steak à la Tartare, Garni 4.50
(Our Tartare Steak, garnished)

La Côte de Boeuf Rôtie au Jus 3.50
(Roast Prime Rib of Beef au Jus) (Saturday only)

Les Légumes du Jour --- La Salade à l'Ail ou Chiffonnade
Pain --- Beurre --- Café ou Thé --- Milk 15¢ extra
Glace --- Sorbet --- Patisserie Française --- Pommes ou Pêches au Vin en Saison
Le Gâteau au Rhum --- Le Gâteau aux Amandes
La Meringue Glacée Chantilly 50¢ --- La Coupe aux Marrons 50¢
La Pêche Melba 50¢ --- Le Baba au Rhum 50¢ --- La Coupe François 50¢
La Mousse au Chocolat 45¢ --- L'Ananas au Kirsch 45¢
Le Plateau de Fromage 50¢

friend and master chef Jean Pierre Goyenvalle, the first seating was anything but smooth. Mercifully, a severe thunderstorm knocked out the power, so patrons who arrived later had to be sent home without supper. It immediately became clear that François's popularity had followed him, and his dream would have to be expanded to accommodate his following. From the initial hope of serving seventy-five people a night, and doing all the work ourselves, we now serve twice that number with a staff of more than fifty-five.

At the downtown restaurant, Papa's favorite saying was, "There is only one way to do things around here, my way." He ran the entire operation. At L'Auberge, however, it is definitely a family affair. Though my father is still firmly in control, he tries to balance the enthusiasm and impatience of his three sons with the knowledge and expertise he and my mother have acquired. Papa plans the menus, does the purchasing, cuts the meat, makes the pâtés, supervises the grounds maintenance, and generally keeps his three sons on their toes.

My mother, Marie-Antoinette, never had a chance to make very many pastries, though we use several of her recipes. Writing the daily menu, so that we may offer the freshest seasonal dinners, keeping the books, attending to the numerous administrative details, and helping in the dining room have kept her occupied. Her calm demeanor is a counterbalance to the fast pace and constant pressures in the inner workings of the restaurant.

Number two son, Robert, was with us at the opening. Following this, he took a leave of absence to complete his dining room training in another French restaurant in the area. A few months later he rejoined the business in earnest. Initially, Robert helped Frieda Bene, Papa's right arm, who for many years has been in charge of the Chez François dining rooms. However, my brother soon discovered his preference for *la cuisine* and joined me in the kitchen.

This left the dining room duties to my youngest brother, Paul, who joined us in 1979. Paul's ability to make our customers feel welcome, coupled with the fact that he is the best looking of the three, made him the natural choice to supervise the front of the house. His role is to maintain the friendly ambiance and personal service of Chez François. Paul's arrival completed my father's dream of a family-run *auberge*.

As the *chef de cuisine* my responsibilities include examining the incoming foodstuffs to guarantee that only the freshest ingredients are used by the twenty-member kitchen staff; tasting, appraising, and finishing our cuisine; approving dishes before they are served, and generally ensuring that Papa's instructions are carried out.

The cuisine at L'Auberge includes popular classics enjoyed by our patrons for over thirty years, a few adaptations of regional American dishes, and a number of recipes inspired by recent culinary thought. Still, the emphasis is on the Alsatian specialties from Papa's part of France, the regional cuisine of Alsace being one of the richest and most varied. Our cookery has a far more personal aspect than was possible downtown, and takes full advantage of the many excellent products now found in America, such as fresh *foie gras* and domestic wild mushrooms, which were simply unavailable until recently. Produce from our two herb gardens, a small but growing vegetable garden, and our orchard, all planted by Papa, as well as nearby vegetable farms also figure prominently in our menu. The recipes bear my father's mark, the artists' finishing touch.

In keeping with Papa's tradition of personally overseeing every aspect of preparation, he has reviewed these recipes for accuracy. Although both of us felt that the recipes should detail our exact methods, Papa was concerned that some were too time consuming. "Who is going to go to all that trouble? You must tell them they may use chicken broth in place of *fonds blanc*." This inspired me to include "Monsieur François's hints to the home cook" after most of our recipes. These suggestions for substitutions, variations, and alternate techniques are meant to facilitate the execution of our recipes with the least discernible loss of flavor.

In the early fifties, most of our customers had not adopted the European tradition of drinking wine with dinner. A patron might tell the waitress, "The girls will have Cokes and the boys will have coffee." To encourage patrons to drink wine with their meals, Papa, after a suggestion from his friend Aaron Millman, ordered table tents announcing a recommendation of particular wines. The table tents bore Papa's profile. People began to doodle on these profiles, and so he established a monthly contest for the most amusing caricature. Those included in this book are only a small sampling of many thousands of sketches we have enjoyed over the past thirty years.

François Haeringer: Le Restaurant, C'est Moi

The Unassuming Alsatian Behind Chez François
by William Rice

A baseball or football team usually has a man known as a player's player —he does everything well, and his leadership holds the team together. If there is a restaurant owner's restaurant owner in Washington, he is François Haeringer, the diminutive Alsatian of Chez François.

Haeringer is a man of contradictions. His old world sternness and sense of discipline are offset by a warmth and kindness that often embarrass him. His formal courtesy disguises a dislike of chi chi and pomp. His classical chef's training has surrendered to—or at least bent to—the realities of running a big city restaurant in America.

François, colleagues say with a depth of appreciation usually reserved only for fine wine, is a "restaurateur." A restaurateur doesn't just write pay checks and collect profits: he knows the business, every facet of it, and he can perform any task necessary to insure its continued operation. Some claim François Haeringer is the only man in Washington who deserves that title. No one disputes his right to it.

The outside of François's restaurant at 818 Connecticut Avenue Northwest, is cool and elegant. Its façade could comfortably join those along the streets off the Champs Elysées. Its interior can be found nowhere else. Almost everything used by decorators to create "provincial atmosphere" in restaurants is somewhere in Chez François. A line of artificial flowers rides atop a curved banquette in the main room. There are long-handled pots and plates on the wall, a small roof of clapboard, artificial grapes, and a rack of wine bottles alongside the stairs to the second floor.

The restaurant, fifteen years old this year, is something of an economic miracle. It is no longer cheap, but its complete lunches and dinners are moderately priced. Its French menu, prepared by a staff of American cooks, is the most extensive to be found in a local restaurant. The wine list is varied and costs are below average. Customers wait in line at both lunch and dinner despite the addition last fall of a second floor *auberge*.

The crowded restaurant, which serves more than five hundred meals every day, is situated less than two blocks from the White House. It should be an ideal place to drop names, but François has neither the time or the inclination to do so. Who are the customers? "I don't know," he answers with surprise. "I never ask them really." Then he adds, "It is a good middle-class group, I think, and in the last year or so I have begun to get many more young people."

He is unassuming about the restaurant's success. "I think it is the prices, and the food isn't too bad." He continues, "I don't think the at-

Reprinted with the kind permission of *The Washingtonian* and William Rice, now Editor-in-Chief of *Food and Wine Magazine*. This article appeared in *The Washingtonian* (October 1969).

mosphere is bad either." Then, after a pause, "You know, a lot of people like the girls." (He has a veritable United Nations of waitresses.) "I have a nice crew. They are not for a specialty place. They wouldn't know how to carve a duck or do a crêpe suzette, but I don't ask them to."

François makes two inspection trips a day through his kitchens (the upstairs has its own kitchen). "They line up everything on a table and I taste. I say more sherry, or more cream, or more salt, and my cooks do it. I have no French chefs. If you even go into the kitchen they sulk for eight days. I may have more problems in that I have to check up on things, but this is how I made my success. I tell them, 'Listen, gentlemen, we are artists. We blend things together just like an artist with paints. Be proud of what you do.' "

He administers a staff of eighty-seven and supervises every detail, from the ordering of groceries to the clipping of the hedge around the outside terrace.

Despite the profile sketch of him that appears on a small card at each table (and which has inspired some inventive art work between courses), François is not well-known to his customers. This is due to the size of the restaurant, to modesty, and to a desire to preserve his sanity. "Most of the time I don't work at the door," he says. "I would go nuts with everyone wanting tables. And, frankly, it is very hard for me to refuse somebody." Nor will he recommend specific dishes to customers. "You find the things the kitchen said were good already lined up on plates. It becomes a device to get rid of stuff that must be used up."

François can often be found in the "office." It is a long, narrow space tucked under the stairs on the first floor which holds him only because it is a dead-end alley. Long of nose and short of chin, he bursts into motion as though he were wearing a spaceman's jet backpack. His dress is neat but informal; a ring of at least fifteen keys worn at the belt is his only badge of authority. At fifty, he is well-fed but not fat. His hair is streaked with grey, and the circles under his eyes are testimony to his labors.

He completely dominates Chez François. Questions from the chefs, questions from the hostesses, calls from customers — he fields them all. The menu is his creation. "It has never been shaped by what a customer may want but always by what I want to serve. There are thirty items, so there is plenty of choice. When I start a new dish, I send samples to customers I know. That's how I advertise."

The decor? François brought the decorative pieces from home, from Alsace. This one-man rule is, in fact, the restaurant's greatest weakness. No one else is strong enough to hold the place together without him. "When he goes away more than a week or so, things go off," a hostess confesses, "and he has to come back before it goes right again."

Things have been that way since 1954, when François, then chef at the Three Musketeers, took over operation of the restaurant from

Henry Ambord and changed its name from the Three Musketeers to Chez François.

In the beginning there were two rooms which seated about seventy-five. François, who owns the restaurant name but leases the space from the Claridge Hotel, added what had been the King Cole room to his domain in 1959. Last year's second floor expansion provided a much needed bar for waiting customers and increased seating capacity to 250. His role as proprietor of a second restaurant ended three years ago when he sold Le Gourmet, now the Club. "It is not good to have two businesses," he says, shaking his head and hitting the table with an outspread hand.

Still, what he has is enough to qualify him as one of the most successful native sons of Obernai, the Alsatian town (populaton 4,851) whose local wine still finds a place on his list. He was the first male baby born there after Alsace became French at the end of World War I. Hence François.

As a boy he read of the life of a cook in America in letters from his older Brother Alfred, who had come to Washington to join their chef-uncle Jacques Haeringer. Alfred (Freddy) is still here and operates Haeringer's Buffeteria in Silver Spring. Jacques, who died in 1953, opened the old Shoreham in 1911 and went on to supervise the kitchens at the Carlton, the Mayflower, and the Chevy Chase Club.

François's father, a businessman with assorted interests, was agreeable when his youngest son, age sixteen, decided to make his career in the kitchen. "My brother was writing from America how good it was. I liked to fiddle around in my mama's kitchen."

His father paid to have him apprenticed at a hotel in nearby Kaysersberg, where he rose at 4 a.m. to help clean the kitchen. One of his chores was sifting ashes from the stove and scattering them over wine bottles in the cellar. "It was slavery," he admits without bitterness. "I cried a lot, but I learned."

After three years in Kaysersberg and Strasbourg, he went to Paris and the kitchen of the highly regarded Plaza-Athenée. Then came World War II, service in the French Army, capture by the Germans, and, as an Alsatian, "liberation." Faced with the prospect of being liberated into the German Army, François chose instead to ply his trade at the Four Seasons, a prestige hotel in Munich.

The chef at the Four Seasons was Alfred Walterspiel, whom François calls the "German Escoffier." Walterspiel's reputation drew top Nazis to the Four Seasons. The chef, along with his young assistant, was commandeered on several occasions to cook at the nearby headquarters of the S.S. According to François, "I went six times; once when Mussolini was there, another time when Goebbels and Himmler came into the kitchen.

"The oven was in the middle of the kitchen. I would stand on one side, Mr. Walterspiel on the other. There were guards all around. We couldn't put our hands in our pockets or go to the bathroom without an escort. S.S. officers, wearing white gloves, would bring what we needed—flour or whatever—on silver trays, then take it away when we had finished."

Eventually the Four Seasons was bombed, and François finished out the war in a factory kitchen.

After the war, he returned to France and hotel cooking. At Superbagneres, a Pyrenees resort, he met the girl who was to become his wife. In 1948 his American immigration visa was granted. He arrived in Washington speaking no English and spent six months working in his brother's first buffeteria, at Fourteenth Street and Delafield Place, Northwest. Then he worked for his uncle at the Chevy Chase Club. When Jacques became ill, François took over as chef. The crew was mostly Italian. Club officials spoke only English. François had no one to talk to but himself.

"I had a hell of a time," he recalls. "Furthermore, someone was stealing. One day I saw the butcher cut a hunk of butter and put it under his shirt. So I ordered him to go to the stove and make some sauces. He couldn't leave. By the time he was finished, the butter was all melted inside his shirt. Then I fired him."

The association with his uncle taught him how to cook for Americans. "Uncle taught me how to make Boston clam chowder. Three times one Saturday he took the pot and threw the chowder on the floor for me to clean up. But I learned."

In 1950 he left Washington, thinking he was to take over the kitchen of a resort hotel in Pennsylvania. The owner convinced him instead to help run another of his hotels, one located in Ketchikan, Alaska. François says he loved the frontier wilderness. But his wife didn't, and following the birth of their first son he decided to leave. Financial difficulties prevented the opening of a Chez François in Ashtabula, Ohio, so he continued back to Washington and the Three Musketeers.

He has lived in Arlington for the past decade with his wife, three sons, a flock of canaries that once numbered 250, a garden, and a large stamp collection.

His eating habits astonish would-be gastronomes. "How much I eat depends on how nervous I am. I have a good lunch, but some days you taste and taste until you don't have any more taste. I am the easiest man to please with food. Some nights I watch TV and eat fresh bread with Spam and drink a glass of beer."

His favorite restaurant is Trader Vic's. "I feel at home there. You know it is one of the best places in town. The service is good and they have a method . . . That's rare." Among the French restaurants, he admires Chez Camille and Sans Souci. "I go over there sometimes to relax," he says.

He is a determined conversationalist, quick to laugh and joke, earnest and eager to return to subjects that concern him, such as labor problems or what to do about taking reservations. He cannot understand the American attitude toward the kind of work that must be done in a restaurant. "Someone has to do the little things," he protests. "Not everyone can go to college or university. If not, you should learn a trade."

The monologue is carried on in snatches. There is a crash in the kitchen. He winces, tries to stay still, can't, and goes off with a quick apology. He returns, has a bite of food, then is cautioning a waitress about pouring too much wine into a glass. Customers pause to thank him. From behind, one of his chefs looms up with a problem.

Because it is late, the staff is bidding him good night. "When they come in, they say 'Good morning,' " he explains proudly. "When they go out, they say 'Good night.' This is something I insist on. I have no clock here. They have no numbers."

On Saturday afternoon, although the restaurant is closed, he is harried. He sits at his desk, a trowel, hedge clippers, light bulbs, an order form for wine, a bunch of bananas, and a salt and pepper shaker set all vying for his attention.

He jokes, plans the menu, and takes reservations. He should say no; he means to. But frequently he can't, and ends up trying to fit in extra customers.

He has two chefs. Roosevelt Little, slender and quick, has been with François since the beginning. Charlie Fowler, large and serious, has been at Chez François and Le Gourmet for ten years. With them François is the patient teacher, the encouraging preacher. Maxims—slogans to live and cook by—come naturally in his accented English.

"Monsieur François is often very hard, very strict," a hostess says. "But that is how he makes his business work. When the tension is off, we all laugh together and he is friendly with everyone. If something is wrong, he is mad and you get it. But once he is through, he is through. He can't keep things to himself, that's just the way he is. He talks to everybody just the same; he listens to their troubles and will try to help them. He is good-hearted. He doesn't want to admit it; he will deny it. But he is good-hearted."

One thing he will admit: "Sometimes now I envy people who go home at 4:30 or 5 and have no worries until tomorrow morning. I guess it's age sneaking up."

This mood, like others, passes. He has a farm near the Potomac in Virginia and plans to go there when he retires to tend the fruit trees. In the meantime, Chez François and its customers are not just obligations. They are his life.

Les Potages

Soups

Soupe à l'oignon gratinée

Onion Soup

This soup, on the menu since 1953, is an all-time favorite, popular both summer and winter.

Serves 8

2 tablespoons butter
3 cups thinly sliced onions
2 tablespoons flour
2 quarts *fonds blanc* (page 42)
¾ tablespoon salt
¼ tablespoon freshly ground pepper
16 ½-inch slices French bread
8 tablespoons grated Gruyère and Parmesan cheese combined

Melt the butter in a heavy saucepan or a Dutch oven. Add the prepared onions and cook slowly, 30 to 40 minutes, over low heat until golden brown, stirring often.

When the onions are browned, stir in the flour, and add the *fonds blanc*, blending it in vigorously with a whisk. Bring the soup to a full boil. Reduce heat and simmer for about 30 minutes. Taste for seasoning and add salt and pepper as needed.

Split a loaf of French bread in half, lengthwise, and cut into ½-inch slices. Place the slices on a baking sheet and brown lightly in a 375-degree oven for 5 to 8 minutes.

Pour the soup into ovenproof bowls. Cover the surface with the prepared croutons and top with the grated cheese. Use 1 heaping tablespoon per bowl. Place the filled bowls under the broiler or in a very hot oven to melt and brown the cheese. Serve immediately.

Monsieur François's hint to the home cook: At L'Auberge we have ample bones with which to make stocks. You may substitute water or beef broth and still obtain acceptable results.

Crème de Champignons

Cream of Mushroom Soup

Serves 6

3 tablespoons butter
2 tablespoons finely minced shallots or onions
1 pound finely chopped mushrooms
4 tablespoons flour
1 quart *fonds blanc* (page 42)
1 teaspoon salt
½ teaspoon freshly ground pepper
1 cup light cream
¼ cup sherry

Melt 2 tablespoons of the butter in a heavy 4-quart saucepan. Add the shallots and soften for 1 minute. Then add the mushrooms and sauté over high heat, stirring often for 10 minutes.

Stir in the flour and add the *fonds blanc* with the salt and pepper. Bring to a full boil. Reduce heat and simmer partly covered for 45 minutes.

Add the cream and remove from heat. Stir in the sherry and remaining 1 tablespoon butter. Adjust seasonings.

Serve with croutons (page 159).

Potage Rouennais

Duck Soup
A Monsieur François Original

Serves 6

2 tablespoons butter
½ cup sliced onions
⅓ cup sliced carrots
¼ cup sliced leeks
2-inch piece of celery
2 duck carcasses
2 quarts water or chicken stock
3 cloves
2 bay leaves
¼ teaspoon thyme
¼ teaspoon cracked black peppercorns (see hint below)
2 tablespoons tomato purée
3 tablespoons flour mixed with ½ cup water
⅓ cup heavy whipping cream
¼ cup sherry
2 tablespoons *duxelles,* optional (page 159)

Melt the butter in a heavy saucepan over medium heat, stir in the onions, carrots, and celery, cover, and simmer for approximately 5 minutes, or until the onions are transparent. Chop the duck carcasses into several pieces with a cleaver and add to the vegetables. Add the water and bring to a boil. Reduce heat and skim off fat. Add cloves, bay leaves, thyme, pepper and tomato purée. Simmer approximately 1½ hours, reducing liquid by one-third.

Blend flour-water mixture into the soup with a whisk. Simmer another ½ hour. Strain and add heavy cream, sherry, and *duxelles.*

Taste and adjust seasonsings if necessary.

Serve with croutons (page 159).

Monsieur François's hint to the home cook: Place the black peppercorns on a hard work surface and crack them by pressing down and forward with the edge of a heavy pan.

Use the leftover duck carcasses from the *Caneton du Long Island Bigarade* recipe (page 116).

Our Boston Clam Chowder

Shortly after arriving in the United States in 1948, François joined his Uncle Jacques, former *chef saucier* under Escoffier in London, and then executive chef at Washington's Chevy Chase Country Club. Uncle Jacques trained in the "old school" and was a very stern perfectionist. One morning he asked François to prepare Boston Clam Chowder, a New England soup that François had never even heard of. Uncle Jacques explained the method and went on to his other duties.

François labored over that soup, knowing his work would be thoroughly scrutinized. Uncle Jacques returned, tasted the soup, frowned, angrily picked up the pot, and poured its contents on the floor. Scolding François, he shouted further instructions, chiding Papa to begin again, *et vite vite*. Twice more the chowder was mopped up from the kitchen floor. Finally, the fourth pot met with Uncle Jacques's approval. My father has never forgotten his introduction to regional American cooking, or the proper way to prepare Boston Clam Chowder *à la française*.

Serves 6

12 large or 18 small hard-shelled clams (Little Necks)
3 cups water
1 *bouquet garni* consisting of 1 bay leaf, 2 cloves, 2 sprigs of parsley, and 5 cracked black peppercorns (see hint on page 4) wrapped in cheesecloth
4 tablespoons butter
¼ cup thinly sliced leeks (bulbs only)
¼ cup minced onions
¼ cup diced celery
3 tablespoons all-purpose flour
½ tablespoon salt
¼ teaspoon freshly ground pepper
⅛ teaspoon thyme
½ cup peeled potatoes, finely diced
2 tablespoons diced green pepper
1 teaspoon chopped garlic
1 teaspoon finely diced bacon
2 dashes Tabasco sauce
1 cup heavy cream

Rinse the clams well under cold running water. Then place them in a heavy 3-quart saucepan. Add the water and the *bouquet garni*. Boil over high heat until the clams open completely. Drain and reserve the broth. When cool enough to handle, remove the clams from the shells, mince, and set aside.

In a heavy saucepan, melt 2 tablespoons of the butter. Add the leeks, onions, and celery; and cook, stirring occasionally, for about 5 minutes, or until the vegetables are slightly tender. Thoroughly blend in the flour. Then add the reserved clam broth, salt, pepper, and thyme, stirring vigorously. Bring the soup to a gentle boil. Add the potatoes and simmer for 20 minutes, or until the potatoes are tender.

Blanch the diced green pepper in boiling water for 1 minute.

Chop the garlic and uncooked bacon together to form a paste.

Add the minced clams and green pepper to the soup. Allow the soup to boil for 2 to 3 minutes and remove from the heat. Stir in the bacon-garlic paste, cream, and Tabasco, adjust seasonings and serve.

Monsieur François's hint to the home cook: Substitute canned clams and clam juice for the broth and still enjoy a good soup.

Vichyssoise

Cream of Leek and Potato Soup

A cold version of the classic *potage parmentier*. It was introduced in New York by Chef Louis Diat, a native of Vichy, France, to sustain and soothe us during our often torrid summers. My father worked under Lucien Diat, Louis's younger brother, at the Plaza Athenee in Paris.

Serves 8

4 tablespoons butter
1 onion, peeled and coarsely chopped (approximately 1 cup)
3 leeks, washed well and finely sliced (approximately 1 cup)
2 tablespoons flour
1 quart *fonds blanc* (page 42)
2-inch piece of bacon rind (optional)
2 large potatoes, peeled and sliced (approximately 2½ cups)
1 tablespoon salt
¼ teaspoon freshly ground pepper
1 cup heavy cream
1 tablespoon finely chopped chives or green onion tops
1 tablespoon finely chopped parsley
¼ teaspoon Worchestershire sauce
Pinch of cayenne pepper or dash of Tabasco sauce
½ teaspoon lemon juice
1 tablespoon per serving of croutons (page 159) if served hot

Melt the butter in a heavy pot over low heat. Add the onion and leeks and cook, stirring often, for 10 to 12 minutes; do not brown. Thoroughly stir in the flour, add the stock and bacon rind, and bring to a full boil. Add the potatoes, salt and pepper and simmer until the potatoes are tender, 15 to 20 minutes.

Discard the rind and purée the soup in a food processor or blender; then push through a strainer into a large bowl and chill.

Before serving, blend in the cream with a whisk, and add chives or green onions and parsley, Worchestershire sauce, cayenne pepper, and lemon juice. Taste and adjust seasonings. Top each serving of hot soup with the croutons.

Monsieur François's hints to the home cook: Since it is not always convenient to prepare homemade stocks, consommé or chicken broth may be substituted for the *fonds blanc*.

Use the whole leek to make the soup.

It is very difficult to chop chives or scallions: Begin at the tips and, working right to left, mince them finely with a sharp knife.

6

Potage Santé

Cream of Sorrel Soup

Serves 8

4 tablespoons butter
1 cup coarsely chopped onions
1 cup finely sliced leeks
2 tablespoons flour
1 quart *fonds blanc* (page 42)
2 cups sorrel leaves, stems removed
2 cups diced potatoes
1 tablespoon salt
¼ teaspoon freshly ground pepper
1 cup heavy cream

Melt 3 tablespoons of the butter in a heavy saucepan over low heat. Stir in the onions and leeks and sweat them, stirring often, for 10 minutes; do not brown.

Thoroughly mix in the flour, add the stock, and bring to a boil over high heat.

Wash the sorrel, remove the stems, and coarsely chop the leaves.

Add the sorrel, potatoes, salt, and pepper and boil gently until the potatoes are cooked through, 15 to 20 minutes.

Purée the soup, return to the saucepan, and heat. Blend in the remaining 1 tablespoon of butter and the cream with a whisk. Adjust the seasonings and serve with croutons (page 159).

Monsieur François's finishing touch: Add a fine julienne of sorrel leaves or some chopped parsley to the soup just before serving.

Crème - Argenteuil

Cream of Asparagus Soup

Serves 4

1 pound of fresh jumbo asparagus
1 quart boiling water
1 tablespoon salt
5 tablespoons butter
¼ cup chopped onions
¼ cup minced leeks, washed well (use all parts)
3 tablespoons all-purpose flour
Freshly ground pepper to taste
¼ cup heavy cream
¼ teaspoon chopped parsley

Wash, peel, and snap off the lower stalks of the asparagus. Reserve the peelings and lower stalks.

Lay the asparagus in a deep pan, so that the tips are facing in the same direction. Cover with the boiling water seasoned with salt. Cook for 5 to 7 minutes, or until the asparagus is tender but still crisp.

Lift the asparagus from the boiling water and plunge into ice water. Reserve the cooking liquid. Only one-quarter of this asparagus is used in the soup. (Serve the remaining pieces with vinaigrette, as a salad, or with melted butter as a side dish.)

Cut the tips from one-quarter of the cooked asparagus, reserving both stalks and tips for the soup. Melt 3 tablespoons of the butter in a heavy 3-quart saucepan. Stir in the onions and leeks, and cook over low heat for 5 minutes, but do not brown. Dust the onions and leeks with the flour and mix thoroughly. Pour in the reserved liquid, blending vigorously with a whisk. Add the raw asparagus peelings, lower stalks, and the reserved cooked stalks. Season with the pepper. Cover and boil gently for 30 minutes.

Purée the soup in a blender or food processor (may have to be puréed in several batches) and force through a fine strainer.

Before serving, reheat the soup and with a whisk stir in the remaining 2 tablespoons of butter and the cream. Adjust seasonings. Add the reserved asparagus tips and garnish with croutons (see page 159) and freshly chopped parsley.

Monsieur François's hints to the home cook: Most soups may be prepared ahead of time, but do not add the cream or butter until ready to serve.

Prepare cauliflower soup, *Crème Dubarry*, in the same manner. Cook one head of cauliflower. Purée half into the soup and serve the remainder as a side dish.

Potage Sauté

Potage Esaü

Lentil Soup

Serves 8

2 cups lentils
½ stick butter plus 1 tablespoon
½ cup chopped onions
⅓ cup chopped carrots
2 thick strips bacon, diced
2 tablespoons flour
2½ quarts *fonds blanc* (page 42)
1 tablespoon salt
¼ teaspoon freshly ground black pepper
½ cup light cream
2 links (¼ pound) frankfurters or smoked pork sausage

Place lentils in a large bowl, cover with water, and soak overnight.

Drain and discard water.

In a heavy 3-quart stockpot, melt the ½ stick of butter, add the onions, carrots and bacon. Simmer for 5 minutes, stirring occasionally. Mix in the flour. Add the *fonds blanc,* blending the ingredients vigorously with a whisk. Add the lentils, salt, and pepper. Bring to a boil and simmer 45 minutes to 1 hour, or until lentils are very soft.

Purée the soup in a blender or food processor (may have to be processed in several batches). Return to pot.

Reheat soup, add cream, and adjust seasonings.

Slice the sausages into thin rounds. In a small skillet, melt the 1 tablespoon butter (do not brown) and lightly sauté the sausage rounds. Add to the soup and serve with croutons (page 159).

Monsieur François's hint to the home cook: Substitute diced country ham for the sausage rounds. A drop of red wine vinegar, added just before serving, enhances the flavor.

Potage de Légumes Frais de l'Auberge

Fresh Vegetable Soup

Serves 8

½ stick butter
¾ cup medium-diced onions
¾ cup medium-diced carrots
¾ cup medium-diced celery
¾ cup medium-diced leeks
2½ quarts *fonds blanc* (see page 42)
¾ cup string beans, sliced small
¾ cup medium-diced potatoes
⅓ cup rice
⅓ cup spaghetti, broken into 1-inch pieces
⅓ cup chopped tomatoes
¾ cup medium-diced turnips
1 tablespoon salt
¼ teaspoon freshly ground pepper
½ teaspoon minced fresh garlic
½ teaspoon very finely diced uncooked bacon
Drop or two of Tabasco sauce

Melt the butter in a heavy 4- or 5-quart saucepan. Add the onions, carrots, celery, and leeks; cover and cook slowly over low heat for 15 minutes, stirring occasionally. Do not brown the vegetables. Pour in the stock and gently boil until all the vegetables are partially tender, about 45 minutes.

Add the string beans, potatoes, rice, spaghetti, tomatoes, turnips, salt, and pepper. Simmer for 30 minutes, or until the potatoes are tender.

Chop the garlic and uncooked bacon together to form a paste. Remove the soup from the heat and stir in the bacon-garlic paste. Add the Tabasco, adjust seasonings and serve.

Monsieur François's finishing touch: Add a few drops of Worcestershire sauce, a tablespoon of heavy cream, and fresh chopped parsley or chives to each portion of soup just before serving.

Crème Andalouse

Tomato Bisque

Serves 6

2 tablespoons butter
½ cup diced leeks, white bulbs only
½ cup coarsely diced onions
¼ cup coarsely diced carrots
1 tablespoon diced celery
4 tablespoons all-purpose flour
1 quart water
10 medium tomatoes, stems removed and quartered
1 cup diced potatoes
4 cloves
2 bay leaves
1 tablespoon salt
¼ teaspoon cracked black peppercorns (see hint on page 4)
1 tablespoon sugar
1 tablespoon red wine vinegar
¾ cup heavy cream
1 tablespoon freshly chopped basil

Melt the butter in a heavy 3-quart saucepan. Add the leeks, onions, carrots, and celery. Let the vegetables simmer covered about 10 minutes, but do not brown. Mix in the flour, blending well.

Add the water, tomatoes, potatoes, cloves, bay leaves, salt and pepper. Bring to a boil, reduce the heat and simmer for 1½ to 2 hours. Remove the bay leaves.

Purée in the blender or food processor. Pour back in the pan. Before serving, reboil and add the sugar, vinegar, cream, and basil. Adjust the seasonings.

Monsieur François's hint to the home cook: Prepare this soup during the late summer and fall using overripe tomatoes. It is excellent served hot or cold.

Bisque de Crevettes

Shrimp Bisque

Serves 6

1 quart *court bouillon* (page 36)
1½ pounds raw shrimp with shells
1 tablespoon olive oil
½ cup diced onions
½ cup pared, diced carrots
½ cup leeks, well washed and cut in slivers
¼ cup diced celery
1 cup dry white wine
2 tablespoons tomato paste
2 bay leaves
3 sprigs parsley
¼ teaspoon tarragon leaves
4 cloves
8 cracked black peppercorns (see hint on page 4)
2 cloves garlic, crushed
2 tablespoons minced shallots
½ cup heavy cream
2 tablespoons sherry
1 tablespoon cognac
2 tablespoons butter
Pinch of cayenne pepper
Beurre manié consisting of 2 tablespoons soft butter and 2 tablespoons all-purpose flour

Bring the *court bouillon* to a rolling boil and add the shrimp. As soon as the liquid boils again, the shrimp are cooked. Remove from the liquid at once and reserve the broth. When the shrimp are cool enough, peel and reserve the shells. Store the peeled shrimp in one cup of the broth and refrigerate for later use.

Heat the olive oil in a heavy 3-quart saucepan. Add the prepared vegetables and sauté until lightly browned. Add the shrimp shells and cook for 3 to 4 minutes, stirring often. Pour in the wine and bring to a boil. Then add 3 cups of the reserved broth, the tomato paste, herbs and spices, shallots, and garlic. Boil gently for 30 minutes.

Prepare the *beurre manié* by blending the flour into the softened butter with a table fork. Stir the mixture into the broth with a whisk and simmer for an additional 15 minutes. Pour the soup through a fine strainer into another pan. Add the cream, sherry, cognac, butter and cayenne. Adjust seasonings. Serve hot.

Monsieur François's hints to the home cook: Since only the shrimp shells are required, you may save the shells from other shrimp dishes and store them in the freezer until enough have accumulated to prepare the bisque. You may prepare lobster, crab, or crayfish bisque using the same recipe.

Les Hors d'œuvres

Appetizers

Cottage Cheese Spread

While visiting Paris once, I decided to spend a few days gaining some bread-making experience at the *boulangerie* of our friend Monsieur Weber. The *chef boulanger*, an affable Spaniard named Juan, seemed to enjoy answering my queries. Several times he took me through the entire process of mixing, kneading, rising and baking. Then he supervised as I hesitantly began to copy his routine.

We made bread throughout the day. The finished loaves were bagged and immediately sent upstairs to replenish the display cases in the boutique. Many of M. Weber's customers purchased bread before each meal, and seeing each one walk out of the shop with a fresh loaf tucked under his arm was for me the perfect image of a Frenchman.

Midmorning the following day, Juan instructed me to carry on alone while he stepped out to the corner *bistro*. Watching me work had no doubt parched his throat. One batch of bread was baking, another proofing, and a third was beginning the cycle in the mixer. Everything seemed normal, if a little hectic, during Juan's absence. I managed to complete an entire batch by the time he returned and I was feeling rather proud.

Suddenly M. Weber shouted from upstairs, "Jacques! You forgot the baker's signature!" In my haste, I had neglected to slash each loaf three or four times with a razor before baking. The cuts release the glutenous tension, allowing the dough to rise more. This gives the loaf its characteristic look.

Embarrassed, I quickly suggested that despite its unorthodox appearance, M. Weber should display the bread, charge an additional 10 centimes per loaf, and explain that it was American style. After all, American jeans were all the rage. Why not American bread? However, he failed to grasp this brilliant marketing concept, and my lunch for the next several days was good ole *pain américain*!

Serves 10

1 pound small-curd, cream-style cottage cheese
⅔ cup sour cream
½ teaspoon salt
¼ teaspoon freshly ground pepper
1 teaspoon finely minced garlic
1 tablespoon finely minced onion
1 tablespoon finely minced green onions
1 teaspoon finely minced chives or parsley

Using a wire whisk, blend the cottage cheese and sour cream well in a small mixing bowl. Add the remaining ingredients. Mix thoroughly and adjust seasonings. Cover the bowl and chill well before serving.

Monsieur François's hint to the home cook: An Alsatian tradition often served with boiled potatoes. Serve it with a basket of warm French bread as an accompaniment to an apéritif.

Quiche Alsacienne

Ham, Bacon, and Cheese Tart
Papa's Hometown Version

Serves 8

1 9-inch baked pie shell (page 166)
4 eggs
1 cup milk
1 cup heavy cream
½ teaspoon salt
Pinch of freshly ground pepper
⅛ teaspoon nutmeg
Pinch of cayenne pepper
1 teaspoon finely minced chives
4 tablespoons butter
¼ cup very finely chopped onion
⅓ pound lean ham, diced
⅓ pound lean bacon, diced
1 teaspoon finely minced shallots
½ cup grated Gruyère cheese
½ cup grated Parmesan cheese

Preheat oven to 375 degrees.

Beat the eggs in a mixing bowl. With a whisk, blend in the milk, cream, salt, pepper, nutmeg, cayenne, and chives. Set aside.

Melt 2 tablespoons of the butter in a heavy skillet over low heat. Add the onions and cook, stirring often, until lightly browned. Remove from the pan and reserve.

Wipe out the pan, melt the remaining 2 tablespoons of butter, and sauté the ham and bacon over medium-high heat until the bacon begins to brown. Add the shallots and the reserved onions, and toss several times with ham and bacon. Drain the rendered fat.

Spread the contents of the pan evenly into the pie shell and sprinkle the cheese on top of the meat.

Fill the pie shell with the batter and bake 30 to 40 minutes, or until a knife inserted into the center of the custard comes out clean and the top is golden brown.

Remove from the oven and let stand 10 to 15 minutes before cutting.

Monsieur François's hint to the home cook: If prepared in advance, reheat the quiche by covering it with foil and placing it in a 350-degree oven for 10 to 12 minutes.

*Tranche de Foie gras
de Canard aux Reinettes*

Duck *Foie Gras* with Apples

Serves 4

1 cup apple duck sauce (page 48) or orange sauce (page 47)
1 large apple
4 tablespoons butter
1 teaspoon sugar
8 slices white bread
½ pound fresh *foie gras de canard*
Salt and pepper to taste
Flour

Preheat oven to 250 degrees.
   Heat the apple duck sauce, set aside, and keep warm.
   Peel, core, and cut the apple into 8 wedges.
   In a small skillet, melt 2 tablespoons butter over medium-high heat and add the apple wedges. Sprinkle them with the sugar and sauté, tossing occasionally, for 3 to 4 minutes, allowing the sugar to caramelize slightly. Set aside.
   Toast the eight slices of bread and trim away the crusts. Cut four pieces of the toast in half, diagonally. Place the four remaining whole pieces in the center of each of four ovenproof plates. Surround each whole piece of toast with two pieces of apple and two toast wedges, alternating around the plate. Put the four plates into the warm oven.
   Using a sharp knife dipped in hot water, cut the *foie gras* into four equal portions. Lightly salt, pepper, and dust with flour, brushing off any excess.
   Melt the remaining 2 tablespoons of butter in a large skillet over medium heat. Just as the butter begins to brown, carefully add the prepared slices of *foie gras* and cook them for 10 seconds per side. Do not overcook (the liver should be pink inside).
   Remove the plates from the oven and carefully transfer each slice of *foie gras* onto the top of a piece of toast. Pour one-quarter of the warm sauce around each plate and serve at once.

   Monsieur François's hints to the home cook: *Foie gras* now can be readily obtained in gourmet shops. In addition to the domestic type, *mi-cuit* (partly cooked) duck *foie gras* from France is available. It is cylindrically shaped and wrapped in aluminum foil. Both types may be kept refrigerated for several days. I do not recommend the canned *pâté mousse* or the *bloc* of *foie gras* for this recipe. Fresh sautéed *foie gras* is wonderful even without sauce.

Langue de Veau Ravigote

Veal Tongue with Ravigote Sauce

Serves 4

1 veal tongue
2 quarts water
2 tablespoons all-purpose flour
½ onion
½ carrot
2-inch piece of celery
2 tablespoon red wine vinegar
2 bay leaves
2 cloves
¼ teaspoon cracked black peppercorns (see hint on page 4)
1 tablespoon salt
Ravigote sauce (page 54)

Place the tongue in a large bowl, cover with cold water, and refrigerate overnight. The next day, drain off the water and discard.

Using a 3-quart saucepan, pour in the 2 quarts of cold water, and vigorously blend in the flour with a whisk so that no lumps form. This keeps the tongue from discoloring. Place the tongue in the water and add the remaining ingredients. Bring to a boil, lower the heat, cover, and simmer for 2 hours. Test with a large meat fork for doneness. The fork slips out easily when the tongue is pierced deep into its middle.

Remove the tongue from the liquid and allow it to cool until it can be handled easily. Then skin the tongue. (Do not allow it to become cold before skinning, or this task will be very difficult.) Trim the bones and cartilage from the base of the tongue. Then cut thin diagonal slices, beginning at the tip and working back to the base. Arrange the slices of tongue on warm plates and coat with the ravigote sauce just before serving.

Monsieur François's hint to the home cook: If the tongue is cooked ahead of time, it should be stored and then reheated in its own broth. The tongue must remain completely submerged in the broth during cooking and storage to prevent discoloration. Place a small towel over the tongue, allowing the cloth to drape into the broth during cooking and storage.

17

Pâté Campagnard

Country Pâté

This recipe was a challenge to write down. Papa prepares all the pâté himself. He never measures; he just adds a pinch of this and a dash of that until the flavor seems right. A recipe is merely a guide, he says. The many variables, such as freshness, ripeness, and so on must be anticipated by the cook. The chef must look, taste, and think to make a recipe work.

Serves 25 to 30

1½ pounds boneless veal
1 pound pork butt
1 pound fresh pork belly
⅓ cup pistachios (optional)
½ cup sherry
½ teaspoon minced garlic
1 tablespoon salt
½ teaspoon freshly ground pepper
2 eggs, beaten
1 tablespoon powdered gelatin
¾ tablespoon pâté spices (page 20)
¼ cup heavy whipping cream
1 pound fresh pork fatback, thinly sliced (to line mold)

Marinade:

¾ cup sliced onions
⅓ cup chopped carrots
1 2-inch piece of celery
2½ cups dry white wine
½ teaspoon salt
¼ teaspoon cracked black peppercorns (see hint on page 4)
1 sprig fresh parsley
2 bay leaves
2 cloves
1 pinch thyme leaves
½ teaspoon tarragon leaves
2 tablespoons minced shallots
½ teaspoon minced garlic
½ teaspoon pâté spices (page 20)

Slice ¼ pound of the veal and ½ pound of the pork butt into ¼-by-1-inch slivers. Cut the rest of the meat into 1-inch cubes. Place the cubed meat and slivered meat in separate bowls.

Prepare the marinade. Strain enough marinade over the slivered meat to barely cover. Combine the cubed meat and the remaining marinade. Cover the bowls and refrigerate overnight.

Add the pistachio nuts to the sherry and let stand overnight as well.

The following day finely grind the cubed meat and vegetables with their marinade.

18

In a large bowl, combine the ground meat mixture with the slivered meat and its marinade. Add all the other ingredients, including the pistachio mixture, and mix thoroughly. Test for seasoning by forming a small patty and frying it in butter over low heat. Allow meat to cool. Adjust seasonings if necessary. (Overseason slightly as the pâté will be served cold.)

Line a 12-cup stoneware or aluminum loaf pan with the fatback. Pour in the mixture, cover with fatback, and place one bay leaf in the center.

Preheat oven to 375 degrees.

Pour approximately 1 inch of water into a roasting pan and set on the stove over high heat. Place the pâté in the pan and bring the water to a boil. Transfer the pan to the oven and cook the pâté for 1¾ hours. The water should just simmer; check the level after 45 minutes and add more boiling water if necessary. The pâté is cooked when a meat thermometer registers 160 degrees.

Remove the pâté from oven and water bath. The pâté should be weighted in order to keep the loaf compact and to facilitate slicing. Cover the pâté with foil and place a board, cut to fit, inside the rim of the mold. Two 10- to 15-ounce cans will serve as weights. Cool for 2 to 3 hours and then refrigerate.

Allow pâté to rest 2 days before serving.

Monsieur François's hints to the home cook: Equal portions of nutmeg and cinnamon may be used instead of the pâté spice mixture. After filling the pâté mold, tap it on the counter to settle the ingredients and remove any air pockets.

Épices Composés

Pâté Spices

My father personally prepares all the pâtés served at L'Auberge. This is without a doubt his favorite task. His mother's family operated a *charcuterie* for generations in his home town of Obernai, Alsace, a province renowned for its pâtés and sausages. Papa often reminisces that he would have joined the family business had it not been for the frigid working conditions in the butcher shop.

While in France, I spent the fall with my cousins learning the finer points of cold weather survival techniques in *la charcuterie*, where for hygienic reasons low temperatures are required in meat preparation areas. How did my co-workers endure the numb fingers and frozen feet? Promptly at 6 a.m., after two hours of work, a bottle of schnapps, another Alsatian specialty, was passed around. The effects lasted until 9 when we ate a hearty breakfast of freshly made sausages, country bread, and steaming coffee.

This recipe has been used for generations by our cousins, the Ohressers, in their *Charcuterie*, Rue du General Gourand, Obernai, Alsace, Papa's home town.

Makes enough for 8 to 10 pâtés

½ teaspoon powdered bay leaf
½ teaspoon thyme leaves
½ teaspoon mace
¾ teaspoon cinnamon
1 teaspoon nutmeg
1 teaspoon cloves
½ teaspoon white pepper
½ teaspoon rosemary
½ teaspoon basil
Pinch of cayenne pepper

The bay leaf, thyme, rosemary, and basil must be very dry in order to facilitate grinding.

Put all the ingredients through a spice mill or buy them already powdered. Grind all the spices separately, combine in the proper proportions, and mix thoroughly. Sift the mixture through a fine mesh sieve. Store in a tightly sealed container to prevent loss of flavor.

Rillettes de Canard

Potted Duck and Pork

Serves 25 to 30

1 5-pound duck
1½ pounds pork shoulder
1 pound unsalted pork belly
4 tablespoons rendered duck fat or oil
3 cups chopped onions
2 cups dry white wine
6 cups water
1 *bouquet garni* consisting of 6 cloves, 2 bay leaves,
   1 teaspoon cracked peppercorns (see hint on
   page 4), 3 sprigs fresh thyme, 6 crushed coriander seeds,
   and 2 cloves crushed garlic, wrapped in cheesecloth
1½ teaspoons salt
½ teaspoon ground pepper
¼ tablespoon finely minced garlic
⅛ teaspoon ground cinnamon
⅛ teaspoon ground nutmeg
2 tablespoons sherry
1 tablespoon cognac
2 tablespoons chopped parsley

Debone the duck, reserving the bones and sinews for duck stock. Cut the duck—meat, skin, and fat—together with the pork and pork belly into 1-inch cubes.

Preheat oven to 350 degrees.

Heat the duck fat or oil in a heavy pot or large Dutch oven; add all the meat and sauté for five minutes. Mix in the onions and continue cooking another ten minutes, stirring often. Pour in the wine and bring to a boil. Add the water and *bouquet garni* and boil again. Cover the pot and place in the oven. The rillettes must barely simmer for approximately 4½ hours. Stir occasionally. If the mixture boils, reduce oven temperature to 300 degrees. Be sure to keep the pot tightly covered. The meats must cook until they fall apart easily; test with a meat fork.

Remove the pot from the oven and discard the *bouquet garni.* Take a large meat fork and, with a back and forth motion, shred the meats. Thoroughly mix the rillettes to blend the meat and liquids. Stir in the salt, pepper, garlic, cinnamon, nutmeg, sherry, cognac, and chopped parsley. Adjust seasonings. The rillettes must be overseasoned as it will be served cold.

Ladle the rillettes into one large or several small ceramic pots. Cool completely, cover, and refrigerate for 24 hours before serving.

Serve as a spread with warm French bread.

Monsieur François's hint to the home cook: The rillettes and pâtés will keep at least two weeks if sealed with lard or rendered fat (duck or goose). Melt the lard and carefully cover the cooled rillettes with ¼ inch, and refrigerate.

Terrine de Gibier

Venison Terrine

My grandfather Ernest was an avid hunter. One of his trophy roebuck deer heads hangs above the pastry table at L'Auberge. Papa notes that these hunting trips were always followed by huge picnic lunches, high-lighted by pâtés made with game bagged on previous outings. Grandpa knew that the best way to savor venison pâté was outdoors with a group of friends.

Serves 25 to 30

¼ cup pistachios, blanched and peeled (optional)
½ cup port
2 pounds boneless venison (deer)
1½ pounds fresh pork belly
½ pound fresh pork fatback cut into ¼-inch cubes
3 eggs, beaten
½ teaspoon freshly ground pepper
¼ teaspoon ground mace
¼ teaspoon nutmeg
⅛ teaspoon cinnamon
2 tablespoons brandy
1 tablespoon salt
1 clove garlic, finely chopped
3 shallots, finely chopped
1 teaspoon powdered gelatin
1 pound fresh pork fatback, thinly sliced (to line mold)

Marinade:
½ cup sliced onion
1 2-inch piece of celery
2 shallots, finely chopped
2 cups red wine
½ teaspoon salt
¼ teaspoon cracked black peppercorns (see hint on page 4)
1 sprig fresh parsley
1 bay leaf
2 cloves garlic
3 juniper berries, crushed
1 pinch thyme leaves

Prepare the marinade. Cut the venison and pork belly into cubes and marinate overnight in the refrigerator.

Combine the pistachios and the port and let stand overnight as well.

Pass the marinade and entire contents (meat, wine, and vegetables) through a food grinder using the fine disc, or grind in a food processor. Put the mixture in a large bowl and add all other ingredients (including cubed fatback) and mix thoroughly. Fry a small amount and taste for seasoning.

Line a 12-cup terrine—earth or aluminum—with the slices of fatback. Pour in the mixture and cover with fatback.

Preheat oven to 375 degrees.

Pour approximately 1 inch of water into a roasting pan and set on the stove over high heat. Place the terrine into the pan and bring the water to a boil. Transfer the pan to the oven and cook the terrine for 1½ hours. The water should just simmer; check the level after 45 minutes and add more boiling water if necessary. The liver pâté is cooked when a meat thermometer registers 160 degrees.

Remove the terrine from oven and water bath. The terrine should be weighted in order to keep the loaf compact and to facilitate slicing. Cover the terrine with foil and place a board cut to fit inside the rim of the mold. Two 10- to 15-ounce cans will serve as weights. Cool for 2 to 3 hours and then refrigerate.

Allow terrine to rest 2 days before serving.

Monsieur François's hint to the home cook: Technically, the term *pâté* refers to meats baked in dough and *terrines* to those cooked in earthenware or crockery. Today, the terms are used interchangeably.

Terrine de Foie de Canard

Duck Liver Terrine

Serves 25 to 30

1 pound fresh pork shoulder, cubed
1 pound fresh pork belly, cubed
1¾ pounds duck livers, trimmed
3 tablespoons minced onions
6 tablespoons oil
1 teaspoon sugar
½ teaspoon paté spices (page 20)
1¼ tablespoons salt
2 tablespoons heavy cream
½ tablespoon freshly ground black pepper
2 tablespoons cognac
½ cup Madeira
1 bay leaf
2 whole eggs, beaten
½ teaspoon powdered gelatin
1 teaspoon minced garlic
2 tablespoons minced shallots
3 tablespoons chopped parsley
1 pound fresh pork fatback, thinly sliced (to line mold)

In a large skillet over high heat sauté the pork shoulder, pork belly, 1¼ pounds duck livers, and the onions in the oil until lightly browned. This will have to be done in 3 batches. Use 2 tablespoons of oil and 1 tablespoon of onions for each batch. Allow the meat to cool. Then grind all the sautéed meat using a fine disc or a food processor. Place in a large mixing bowl, add the ½ pound of reserved livers, and blend in all the other ingredients. Mix thoroughly and then test for seasoning.

Test by making a small patty and cooking in butter over low flame. Allow meat to cool. Adjust seasonings if necessary.

Line a 12-cup terrine mold with bards (thin slices of fatback). Cover the bottom first and then press bards onto the sides and ends, cutting pieces to fit. Fill three-quarters of the terrine with the liver mixture and cover with the fatback. Place a bay leaf on top of the fatback.

Preheat oven to 375 degrees.

Pour approximately 1 inch of water into a roasting pan and set on the stove over high heat. Place the terrine into the pan and bring the water to a boil. Transfer the pan to the oven and cook terrine for 1½ hours. The water should just simmer; check the level after 45 minutes and add more boiling water if necessary. The liver paté is cooked when a meat thermometer registers 160 degrees.

Remove the terrine from oven and water bath. The terrine should be weighted in order to keep the loaf compact and to facilitate slicing. Cover the terrine with foil and place a board, cut to fit, inside the rim of the mold. Two 10- to 15-ounce cans will serve as weights. Cool for 2 to 3 hours and then refrigerate.

Allow the terrine to rest 2 days before serving.

Monsieur François's hint to the home cook: Remember when adjusting the paté seasoning that the mixture must taste somewhat overseasoned as the patés are served cold.

Pâté Chaud en Croûte

Warm Pâté in Puff Pastry

Serves 6

½ pound pork shoulder
½ pound boneless veal
2 whole eggs
1 teaspoon cognac
2 strips puff pastry, 12 by 5½ by ⅛ inches (page 167)
1 egg, beaten with 1 teaspoon water

Marinade:

⅓ cup white wine
⅓ cup Madeira
2 bay leaves
1 tablespoon finely chopped
  shallots
1 tablespoon minced onion
1 teaspoon minced garlic

Few sprigs of parsley
1 2-inch piece of celery
1 2-inch piece of carrot
1 tablespoon salt
¼ teaspoon freshly ground pepper
¼ teaspoon pâté spices (page 20)

Begin the day before by cutting the meats into 1-inch cubes. In a large bowl, combine the cubed meat with the marinade ingredients. Mix well, cover, and refrigerate overnight.

The following day, grind all the marinated ingredients, including the wine, through a fine disc. Beat the 2 eggs and mix into the ground meat, along with the brandy. Taste for seasoning by forming a small patty and frying it in butter over low heat. Allow the meat to cool, taste, and adjust seasonings if necessary.

Preheat oven to 350 degrees.

Place one strip of the pastry on an ungreased baking sheet and brush a 1-inch band of the egg wash around the rim. Mound the pâté mixture down the center of the strip. Be sure not to put any of the meat onto the egg wash. Cover with the remaining strip of dough and press down firmly to make the edges adhere.

Prepare a "chimney" for the pastry by folding a 2-inch piece of aluminum foil around a pencil. Cut a small hole in the center of the pastry and insert the chimney. This allows the steam to escape.

Brush the entire surface with the remaining egg wash and bake for approximately 40 minutes. The internal temperature when checked with a thermometer should be 160 degrees. If the crust browns too quickly, cover with a tent of foil.

Remove from the oven, slice into six equal portions, and serve with Madeira Sauce (page 40), if desired.

Monsieur François's hint to the home cook: Always use a "chimney" when baking pâté and sausages in puff pastry; otherwise the dough will be soggy.

Tranche à l'oignon

Onions in Puff Pastry
A modern version of the traditional Alsatian onion tart

Serves 4

¾ cup butter
5 cups shredded onions (approximately 3 onions)
1 teaspoon sugar
¼ teaspoon salt
Pinch of freshly ground pepper
½ pound puff pastry (page 167)
⅓ cup shredded Gruyère cheese
2 eggs, beaten

Melt the butter in a small heavy saucepan over low heat. Add the onions and cook slowly until dark brown, 50 to 60 minutes. Stir the onions often, scraping the bottom of the pan to prevent scorching.

Transfer the browned onions to a small mixing bowl and season with the salt, pepper, and sugar. Set aside to cool.

While the onions are browning, roll the puff pastry into a 12-by-10-inch rectangle that is ⅛-inch thick. Trim any excess dough and cut in half lengthwise, forming two 5-by-12-inch bands. Extra puff pastry may be frozen for later use.

Preheat oven to 425 degrees.

Place one band on an ungreased baking sheet and brush a 1-inch strip of egg around the rim. Mound the onions down the center, being careful not to let any overlap onto the egg border. Sprinkle the Gruyère cheese over the onions. Cover with the remaining band of dough and firmly press the edges together.

Prepare a "chimney" for the pastry by folding a 2-inch piece of aluminum foil around a pencil. Cut a small hole in the center of the top layer of pastry and insert the chimney. This allows the steam to escape.

Brush the entire surface with the beaten egg and bake until golden brown, approximately 20 minutes.

Divide the pastry into four equal parts and serve hot.

Paté Chaud en Croute

Feuilleté de Chanterelles

Sautéed Chanterelles in Puff Pastry

Serves 4

12 ounces puff pastry (page 167)
1 egg, beaten
1 cup Madeira sauce (page 40)
¾ pound fresh Chanterelles mushrooms, washed well and drained
3 to 4 tablespoons olive oil
Salt and pepper to taste
1 teaspoon finely minced shallots
Pinch of finely minced garlic
1 teaspoon finely chopped parsley

Preheat oven to 400 degrees.

On a floured surface, roll out the puff pastry into a 5-by-12-inch rectangle approximately ⅛ inch thick. Trim any uneven edges, and cut into four equal strips of dough, each about 3 inches wide.

Turn the strips upside down and transfer to a baking sheet. Wipe off any excess flour and brush the surface of the dough with the beaten egg using a pastry brush. Bake in the preheated oven until golden brown, 12 to 15 minutes. Turn off the oven.

When cool enough to handle, carefully cut the rectangles in half through their centers and place one on each of four ovenproof plates.

Heat the Madeira sauce and keep warm.

Transfer the plates to the warm oven while preparing the mushrooms.

Heat the olive oil in a large skillet, add the chanterelles, and sauté for 4 minutes, tossing occasionally. Season with salt and pepper and sprinkle with the shallots, garlic, and parsley. Toss several times and remove from heat.

Take the plates from the oven and lift off the top halves of the puff pastry. Divide the wild mushrooms, spoon over the bottom halves, and cover with the top half of each pastry. Spoon the Madeira sauce around each *feuillette* and serve.

Monsieur François's hints to the home cook: American wild mushrooms—chanterelles, morels, girolles, cèpes, hedgehog, chicken of the woods, and cauliflower—are plentiful. Mix several varieties for a truly memorable appetizer. Sauté the mushrooms over very high heat. If necessary prepare the mushrooms in several batches as they will not cook properly if overcrowded in the pan.

Feuilleté de Crabe

Crabmeat in Puff Pastry

Serves 4

12 ounces puff pastry (page 167)
1 beaten egg
1 green pepper
2 tablespoons butter
2 tablespoons finely minced shallots
1 cup heavy cream
½ teaspoon lemon juice
½ teaspoon salt
Pinch each of freshly ground pepper and cayenne pepper
1 pound lump crabmeat

Prepare the puff dough and brush with the egg as described in the recipe for sautéed chanterelles in puff pastry on page 27.

Prepare the green pepper by brushing the skin with oil and placing in a 500-degree preheated oven until the skin blisters and turns very dark. When cool enough to handle, rub away all the skin, cut off the stem, split the pepper, and remove the seeds and membrane. Dice the pepper; there should be approximately ⅓ cup.

Set oven to 200 degrees.

Melt the butter in a heavy saucepan. When the foam subsides, add the shallots and sauté for a few moments. Add the diced pepper and cook for 1 minute. Pour in the heavy cream and bring to a full boil. Reduce the cream by boiling for about 4 minutes until thick enough to coat a spoon. Add the lemon juice, salt, pepper, and cayenne, to taste. Remove from the heat.

Split the puff pastries in half lengthwise, place on four ovenproof plates, and set in the warm oven.

Pick through the crabmeat to remove any pieces of shell. Carefully stir the crabmeat into the cream and simmer over low heat for 2 to 3 minutes. Taste and adjust seasonings. The crabmeat should be warmed through but not mashed.

Remove the plates from the oven, lift off the top half of the pastries, and spoon the crabmeat onto each pastry bottom. Replace the tops and serve immediately.

Monsieur François's hint for the home cook: Use top-grade, jumbo lump crab for all your crab dishes. Substitute a dash of Tabasco for the cayenne pepper if you wish.

Ballotine de Sole

Sole Pâté

Serves 10

2½ to 3 pounds boneless and skinless lemon or grey sole fillets
4 to 6 jumbo asparagus
3 tablespoons softened butter
Salt and pepper
2 quarts fish stock (page 37)
Herb mayonnaise (page 53)

Wash the sole fillets and pat dry. Trim any pieces of dark skin that may have been overlooked. Prepare a sole mousse with 1 pound of the fillets using the same recipe and method as in the pike mousse described on page 62. Refrigerate 1 hour before assembling the ballotine.

Parboil the asparagus in salted water until tender but still crisp, 5 to 6 minutes. Drain and reserve.

Butter an 18-by-20-inch sheet of heavy-duty aluminum foil. Place it in front of you so that the long side of the rectangle runs left to right.

Lay 8 to 10 of the remaining fillets white side down on the foil, beginning in the center and working out towards the right and left edges. The fillets should touch but not overlap. A 2- to 3-inch margin of foil should remain at the right and left sides. Lightly season the fish with salt and pepper.

Working left to right, pile half the sole mousse down the center of the fillets. Cut tips approximately 2 inches long off the asparagus stalks and line them end to end down the center of the mousse left to right. Cover the asparagus with the remaining mousse.

Form the ballotine by encasing the fillets and mousse in the foil. Grasp the foil at the bottom right- and left-hand corners, lift and roll forward, tucking the leading edge under the sole fillets. Tie the ballotine to ensure that it will maintain its shape during poaching. Run a piece of kitchen twine over the ends and several times around the length of the pâté.

Fill a deep narrow rectangular pan or fish poacher two-thirds full with fish stock and bring to a boil. Carefully lower the ballotine into the fish stock, cover, and simmer for 35 to 40 minutes. The internal temperature must reach 140 degrees. Remove from the heat, allow the ballotine to cool in the fish stock, and refrigerate overnight. The pâté must be thoroughly chilled before slicing.

Cut into ½-inch-thick slices with a serrated knife. Serve with *crudités* (vegetable salads) and *Sauce Vincent* (page 53).

Monsieur François's hint to the home cook: Use any parboiled vegetable such as green beans or carrots with, or in place of, the asparagus to create colorful patterns in the pâté.

Les Moules à la Pointe de Safran

Steamed Mussels in a Light Saffron Sauce

Serves 4

4½ pounds mussels in shells
2 tablespoons finely minced shallots
¼ stick butter
1 cup dry white wine
1 teaspoon lemon juice
¼ teaspoon saffron filaments
Beurre manié consisting of ¾ teaspoon flour and 1 teaspoon soft butter
½ cup heavy cream
Salt and freshly ground pepper to taste
1 tablespoon chopped parsley

The day before, clean the mussels individually under cold running water by scraping off any clinging barnacles or "beards." Discard any half-opened shells or any unusually heavy ones (which will contain grit). Then put the mussels in a large bowl and cover with 2 quarts of water and 4 tablespoons salt. Set the bowl in the refrigerator overnight.

To prepare, remove the bowl from the refrigerator and drain the mussels. Wash them thoroughly under cold running water, removing any barnacles that may have been missed the day before. Put the mussels into a 3-quart saucepan with a lid. Add the shallots, butter, wine, and lemon juice. Cover the saucepan and bring the wine to a boil over high heat, occasionally shaking the saucepan. Cook for approximately 5 minutes, or until all the mussels are open. Overcooking will toughen the mussels.

Strain all the liquid into a 1-quart saucepan. Add the saffron and bring to a rolling boil. Thoroughly blend the softened butter and flour with a fork and blend the *beurre manié* into the sauce. Boil for 5 minutes. Remove from the heat and add the cream and parsley. Adjust seasonings.

Remove the top shell and thoroughly heat the bottom shell containing the mussel in the sauce. Divide the mussels and sauce between four warm large soup bowls and serve.

Monsieur François's hint to the home cook: The addition of ½ cup flour or cornmeal to the water in which the mussels are soaking will encourage them to feed and thereby degorge any grit.

Les Huîtres Chaudes Chez François

Baked Oysters in Herb Butter

Before the *nouvelle* wave, cooking oysters was considered heresy in France. I remember one of Paris's culinary stars asking my father whether he had ever heard of cooking oysters. This item has been on the menu since 1953.

Serves 4

24 Long Island oysters

Herb butter:
½ cup whole spinach leaves
1½ ounces (2 strips) uncooked bacon
1 pound (softened) plus 1 tablespoon lightly salted butter
2 tablespoons chopped parsley
1 tablespoon lemon juice
Drop of Tabasco sauce
1 teaspoon Worcestershire sauce
½ teaspoon each, finely ground anise seed and fennel seed
½ teaspoon freshly ground pepper
½ teaspoon salt
1 heaping teaspoon each, finely ground garlic and shallots
¼ cup white wine
2 tablespoons fresh bread crumbs
1 tablespoon Pernod

Wash the spinach leaves thoroughly in cold water, lifting them from the water so that the grit remains behind. Then remove the stems and press the leaves into a measuring cup to obtain ½ cup. Drain well.

Melt 1 tablespoon of the butter in a small sauté pan and add the spinach. Let it wilt for 2 to 3 minutes, tossing frequently. Remove from the pan and chop very fine.

Finely chop the bacon and sauté until lightly browned, 2 to 3 minutes.

Whip the softened butter in an electric mixer. Add all of the remaining ingredients and blend thoroughly. Cover and refrigerate until ready to use.

Preheat oven to 400 degrees.

Wash the oysters, open, and lift off the shallow shell. Be sure to wipe the oyster knife clean after opening each oyster. Leave the oysters attached to the bottom (deeper) shell.

Place six oysters on four special oyster platters with hollows to hold them level, or on ovenproof dishes covered with a ½-inch layer of rock salt.

Place a rounded teaspoon of the herb butter on top of each oyster. Set in the oven and bake until the butter is completely melted, 8 to 10 minutes. Serve at once.

Monsieur François's finishing touch: Serve with warm French bread to dunk into the melted herb butter.

La Salade de Poisson Mariné

Marinated Fish Salad

This adaptation of seviche is one of our most popular hors d'oeuvres.

Serves 6

½ pound fresh salmon fillets
½ pound fresh sea scallops
1 teaspoon salt
½ teaspoon pepper
1 teaspoon coarsely ground coriander seeds
1 teaspoon chopped fresh dill
Juice of 8 lemons
Juice of 2 limes
1 head Boston lettuce
2 tablespoons finely minced shallots
2 tablespoons chopped parsley
2 tablespoons chopped green scallions
6 fresh white mushrooms
6 teaspoons olive oil

Slice the salmon into slivers ⅛ inch thick. Wash the scallops under cold running water and slice into rounds ⅛ inch thick. Place the salmon and scallops into separate earthenware or stainless steel bowls. Divide the salt, pepper, coriander, and dill evenly between the two bowls.

Press the lemons and limes (heating them in warm water will greatly increase their yield) and carefully cover the salmon and scallops with the juices. Toss gently to be sure all the slivers are coated with the juice. Cover and marinate for 2 hours in the refrigerator.

Wash the Boston lettuce, drain, and dry completely. Place a bed of lettuce on each of six chilled salad plates.

Place equal portions of salmon on the lettuce, and divide the scallops evenly over the salmon. Top each salad with equal portions of the shallots, parsley, and scallions.

Clean the mushrooms and slice them, crosswise, into thin slivers. Decorate each plate with the mushroom slices.

Pour 1 teaspoon of the oil over each salad to moisten and glaze. Serve.

Monsieur François's finishing touch: Top the salad with a small amount of caviar.

Artichauts Farci au Crabe

Cold Artichokes Stuffed with Crabmeat

Serves 4

4 medium-sized artichokes
2 lemons
2 tablespoons salt
2 quarts water
1 pound lump crabmeat
1 tablespoon chopped parsley
1 cup vinaigrette dressing (page 136)

Using a stainless steel knife, cut the stem off the base of each artichoke, and cut off the top quarter of each globe. Slice one lemon in half and rub the base and top surface of each bulb generously with lemon. This will prevent discoloration. Pull off the tough or dark outer leaves from around the base of each artichoke. Snip off the sharp thorny tips from the remaining leaves with heavy-duty scissors.

Add the salt to the water and bring to a boil in a large saucepan. Squeeze the juice from remaining 1½ lemons and add to the boiling water. Drop in the artichokes. Since they tend to float to the surface, you must weigh them down. The best method is to drape a small towel over the artichokes. Then bring the water back to a boil. Put a lid on the pot and cook for 20 to 25 minutes. The artichokes are done when the base can easily be pierced with a knife.

Remove the artichokes from the liquid with a pair of tongs and place upside down in a colander. Allow the artichokes to cool, and then refrigerate.

To serve: Prepare the crabmeat by carefully removing all pieces of shell. Season lightly with salt, pepper, a few drops of lemon juice, and the chopped parsley.

Working with one artichoke at a time, peel off half of the remaining leaves and arrange in concentric circles around the edge of the serving plate. Grasp the base of the artichoke in one hand and pull off the remaining center leaves together in one bundle with the other hand; set aside. Scrape off and remove the choke with a spoon. Place the artichoke bottom in the center of the plate, surrounded by the leaves. Fill the artichoke bottom with one-quarter of the seasoned crabmeat and cover with the reserved bundle of heart leaves.

Serve with individual dishes of vinaigrette and small plates for the discarded leaves.

Les Fonds et Sauces

Stocks and Sauces

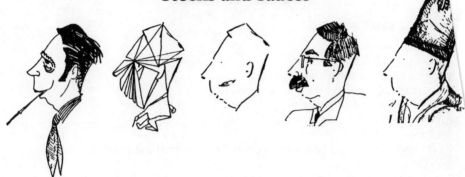

Court Bouillon

Aromatic Broth

Makes 2 quarts

2 quarts water
1 cup onions, cut in slivers
1 cup carrots, cut in thin rounds
½ cup leeks, washed well and sliced
¼ cup celery, cut in slivers
2 bay leaves
3 cloves
½ teaspoon cracked black peppercorns (see hint on page 4)
2 cups dry white wine
2 tablespoons white wine vinegar
2 tablespoons salt

Place all the ingredients in a 3-quart pot and bring to a boil. Reduce the heat and let simmer for 30 minutes, uncovered. Remove from heat and cool.

Transfer liquid and vegetables into a bowl and store in refrigerator until needed.

Monsieur François's hint to the home cook: May be prepared ahead of time or even frozen. Strain the broth to remove the vegetables just prior to use.

— Fumet de Poisson

Fish Stock

My chef said, "Jacques, your nose is the best guide when buying fish. Really fresh fish has a clean, mild sea scent; never a fishy odor." Then, he told me a little story to prove his point.

"Working in a busy seafood restaurant is a sure way to get a seat in the usually crowded subway. At the end of a long day of scaling, filleting and skinning fish in a hot kitchen, I never have a fret about riding a jammed train. One whiff of that unmistakable scent *L'eau de poisson*, and everyone in the metro is eager to step aside. Some are so moved as to stand that I might have an entire bench to myself.

"Jacques, my boy, the nose knows."

Makes 1 quart

½ cup vegetable oil
1 cup onions, peeled and sliced
½ cup carrots, pared and sliced
¼ cup leeks, washed well and sliced
¼ cup celery, sliced
2 pounds fish bones (approximately 5 bass or other non-oily fish)
1 cup dry white wine
1 quart cold water, or enough to completely cover fish bones
1 bay leaf
8 cracked black peppercorns (see hint, page 4)
2 cloves
3 sprigs parsley
2 branches thyme or ¼ teaspoon dried thyme

Heat the oil in a 3-quart stockpot; add the vegetables, cover, and simmer over low heat for about 5 minutes, stirring occasionally, until onion slices are translucent.

Add the fish bones, wine, cold water, and remaining ingredients. Bring to a boil, reduce heat, and simmer uncovered for 25 minutes. Skim as needed.

Remove from heat and strain.

Monsieur François's hint to the home cook: It is important to simmer the fish stock for only 25 to 30 minutes and to strain it immediately to avoid a strong "fishy" taste.

Sauce Américaine

Lobster Sauce

Makes 1 quart

1 live lobster weighing 1 to 1½ pounds
2 tablespoons olive oil
¼ cup each, diced leeks (use all parts), carrots, and onions
1 2-inch piece of celery
2 tablespoons brandy
1 cup white wine
1 quart fish stock (page 37)
2 tablespoons tomato paste
2 cloves each, shallots and garlic
3 bay leaves
5 cloves
½ teaspoon cracked black peppercorns (see hint on page 4)
1 sprig each fresh, or ¼ teaspoon dried thyme and tarragon
½ tablespoon salt
Beurre manié consisting of 2 tablespoons butter and 2 tablespoons flour

Split the lobster's head in half, lengthwise, by inserting the point of a sharp heavy knife where the tail joins the body and cut down through the head. Detach the tail. Remove the claws and crack them with the blunt side of the knife blade. Discard the stomach sac, found in the head. Reserve the green parts (the liver), called tomalley, in a small bowl.

Heat the olive oil in a heavy saucepan over medium heat. Add the vegetables and brown lightly, stirring often.

Add the lobster pieces and juices, and cook until the shell reddens. Add the brandy and ignite. When the flames have subsided, pour in the wine and fish stock. Add the tomato paste, shallots, garlic, and seasonings.

Simmer 15 minutes and then remove the lobster tail and claws. Extract the meat and reserve. Return the shells to the pot and boil for another 30 minutes.

Remove from the heat. Grind the broth and shells in a food processor. This should be done in several small batches, so as not to overtax the machine. If a processor is not available, drain the liquid from the pot and crush the shells with a large ladle or wooden mallet to extract all of the lobster essence. Return the broth and crushed shells to the pot and bring to a boil.

Blend the butter, tomalley, and flour together and whisk this paste into the liquid. Boil another 10 minutes, then force through a fine sieve.

Monsieur François's hint to the home cook: Dot the top of the sauce with butter to prevent a skin from forming.

Fonds Brun Lié

Basic Beef or Veal Sauce

Makes 1 quart

3 pounds veal or beef bones and meat
1 cup coarsely chopped onions
½ cup coarsely chopped carrots
1 2-inch piece of celery
3 tablespoons flour
2 to 2½ quarts cold water
2 tablespoons tomato purée, or 1 fresh tomato, chopped
2 bay leaves
3 whole cloves
Pinch of thyme
4 parsley sprigs (optional)
½ teaspoon cracked black peppercorns (see hint on page 4)
2 cloves garlic, crushed
1 teaspoon butter

Using a meat cleaver, crack and cut the bones into small pieces. Place in a roasting pan and brown in a preheated 375-degree oven for 30 to 40 minutes, stirring occasionally.

Add the onions, carrots, and celery to the partly browned bones and continue cooking until the vegetables are also well browned, approximately 15 more minutes.

Remove pan from oven and drain the fat. Dust the bones with the flour, return pan to the oven, and cook for 5 more minutes.

Transfer the bones and vegetables to a stockpot. Deglaze the roasting pan with 1 cup of the water, scraping any meat particles from the bottom. Cover bones with deglazing liquid and remaining water. Add tomato or tomato purée, herbs, and garlic.

Bring to a boil, reduce heat, and simmer, uncovered, 2½ to 3 hours. Skim occasionally.

Strain into a bowl and discard solids; 2½ to 3 cups of stock should remain. Dot the top of the stock with the butter to prevent a skin from forming.

Monsieur François's hint to the home cook: If a sauce is too thin, the easiest way to thicken it is with cornstarch. Place a small amount in a cup and stir in water, a few drops at a time, until a thick paste (the consistency of kindergarten glue) is formed. Whisk a little into the simmering sauce and boil 2 to 3 minutes. Add more cornstarch until the desired consistency is reached.

Sauce Madère

Madeira Sauce

Serves 4

¼ cup Madeira wine
½ tablespoon finely minced shallots
1 cup *fonds brun* (page 39)
1 tablespoon butter
Salt and freshly ground pepper to taste

In a small saucepan over medium-high heat, reduce the Madeira and shallots by half. Add the *fonds brun*. Bring to a boil and simmer 4 to 5 minutes. Remove from heat and stir in butter with a whisk. Adjust seasonings.
    You may add a little more Madeira just before serving if desired.

Monsieur François's hint to the home cook: substitute sherry or port for the Madeira.

Sauce Charcutière

Brown Sauce with Mustard and Gherkins

Serves 4

½ cup dry white wine
2 tablespoons wine vinegar
1 tablespoon finely minced shallots
1 cup *fonds brun* (page 39)
1 tablespoon Dijon mustard
1 tablespoon butter
1½ tablespoons chopped gherkins
Salt and freshly ground pepper to taste

Place the wine vinegar, wine, and shallots in a small saucepan over high heat and reduce until almost dry. Add the brown sauce. Bring to a boil, reduce heat, and simmer 5 minutes. Remove from heat. Stir in the mustard and butter and add the chopped gherkins. Taste and adjust seasonings.

Monsieur François's hint to the home cook: Enhance the sauce with the addition of fresh chopped herbs such as parsley, chives, or tarragon.

Fonds Blanc

White Stock

Makes 2 quarts

2 chicken carcasses and 2 pounds veal bones and scraps
1 gallon water (approximately)
1 large onion, sliced
2 carrots, sliced
2 leeks, washed well and sliced
1 celery stalk, washed and sliced
2 bay leaves
2 sprigs thyme
4 sprigs parsley
2 cloves
6 cracked black peppercorns (see hint on page 4)

Crack the bones and cut the carcasses into 2 or 3 pieces with a meat cleaver and rinse well in cold water. Place bones in a large stockpot, cover with the water, and bring to a full boil. Skim thoroughly. Add the vegetables and herbs. Reduce heat and simmer, partly covered, for 2 to 3 hours, skimming as necessary.

Pour stock through a fine strainer into a bowl. Chill and reserve.

Monsieur François's hint to the home cook: Remove any congealed fat that accumulates on top of the stock before using.

At L'Auberge we have plenty of bones with which to make stock.

You may substitute consommé, chicken broth, or water for the *fonds blanc* and still obtain acceptable results.

Fonds d'Agneau

Lamb Stock

Makes 1 quart

2 pounds lamb bones and scraps
½ carrot
½ medium onion
2-inch piece of celery
2½ quarts cold water
2 tablespoons tomato purée
3 bay leaves
3 cloves
½ teaspoon thyme
½ teaspoon tarragon
½ teaspoon cracked black peppercorns (see hint on page 4)
1 clove garlic, peeled and crushed

Preheat oven to 450 degrees.

Place the bones and scraps in a roasting pan and brown well for 25 to 30 minutes. Coarsely chop the carrot, onion, and celery. Add these to the bones and cook an additional 15 minutes.

Remove the pan from the oven and transfer the bones and meat to a deep stockpot. Deglaze the roasting pan with 1 cup of the water and scrape any meat particles from the bottom. Cover the bones with the deglazing liquid and the rest of the cold water and bring to a full boil. Skim the broth well and add the remaining ingredients. Lower the heat and simmer 2 to 3 hours. Strain the stock. There should be about 1 quart.

Monsieur François's hint to the home cook: Freeze small quantities in tightly sealed paper cups for later use.

Sauce d'Agneau

Lamb Sauce

Makes 2 to 3 cups

1½ tablespoons minced shallots
1½ tablespoons dry white wine
3 tablespoons red wine vinegar
1 quart lamb stock
3 tablespoons red currant jelly
¾ teaspoon salt
Pinch of pepper

Place the shallots, wine, and vinegar in a heavy 3-quart saucepan. Bring to a full boil over high heat and reduce until nearly dry. Add the lamb stock. Bring to a boil and reduce by one-third. Remove from heat, blend in currant jelly with a whisk, and add salt and pepper. Strain and reserve.

Monsieur François's hint to the home cook: If the sauce is prepared ahead or held overnight, readjust the seasonings before serving.

Fonds de Gibier Lié

Basic Deer Sauce

Makes 1 quart

3 to 4 pounds deer bones and trimmings
3 cups chopped onions (no need to peel)
1½ cups chopped carrots (no need to pare)
2 tablespoons flour
1 gallon water (approximately)
2 tablespoons tomato purée
3 bay leaves
6 whole cloves
Pinch of thyme
4 sprigs parsley
½ teaspoon cracked black peppercorns (see hint on page 4)
2 cloves garlic, peeled and crushed
8 juniper berries, crushed

Using a meat cleaver, crack and cut the bones into small pieces. Place in a roasting pan and brown in a preheated 375-degree oven, turning occasionally, for about 1 hour. Add the onions and carrots to the partly browned bones, and continue cooking until the vegetables are also well browned—about 15 additional minutes.

Dust the bones with the flour, mix well, and transfer the contents of the pan to a large stockpot. Deglaze the roasting pan with 1 cup of the water, scraping any meat particles from the bottom.

Cover the bones with the deglazing liquid and the water. Add the tomato purée, herbs, garlic, and juniper berries. Bring to a boil, reduce the flame, and simmer, partly covered, for 3 to 4 hours. Reduce the stock until 1 quart remains, skimming occasionally. Strain through a sieve and reserve, discarding the solids.

Monsieur François's hint to the home cook: Dot the top of the sauce with butter to prevent a skin from forming.

Fonds de Canard

Duck Stock

Makes 2 cups

2 duck carcasses with necks and giblets
1 large onion, quartered
½ cup carrots, coarsely chopped
2-inch piece celery, chopped
6 cups water (approximately)
½ teaspoon cracked black peppercorns (see hint on page 4)
1 clove garlic, crushed
1 sprig parsley
2 bay leaves
4 cloves
Pinch of thyme

Preheat oven to 400 degress.

Cut the carcasses into 4 or 5 pieces with a meat cleaver and place in a roasting pan with the necks and giblets. Roast in the oven until the bones begin to brown, approximately 20 minutes. Add the onion, carrots, and celery. Roast for another 15 minutes.

Remove the pan from the oven and pour off any fat. Transfer the duck parts and vegetables to a large stockpot. Deglaze the roasting pan with 1 cup of the water and scrape any meat particles from the bottom. Cover the bones with the deglazing liquid and the rest of the water and bring to a boil over high heat. Skim the stock and add all the other ingredients. Lower the heat and simmer, uncovered, for about 2 hours, reducing the liquid by two-thirds. Skim occasionally to remove surface scum.

Strain and carefully degrease before using.

Monsieur François's hint to the home cook: When making stocks, use only enough water to just cover the bones.

Sauce Bigarade

Orange Sauce

Serves 4

2 navel oranges
1 lemon
2 rounded tablespoons sugar
1½ teaspoons red wine vinegar
1 cup duck stock (page 46)
¾ teaspoon cornstarch
1½ teaspoons cold water
1 teaspoon butter
1 teaspoon Cointreau or Curaçao
Salt and freshly ground pepper to taste

Remove the rind from 1 orange and ½ of the lemon with a vegetable peeler. Cut into fine julienne strips. Blanch by dropping the strips into a small pan of boiling water for 3 to 4 minutes. Drain and reserve.

Squeeze the 2 oranges to obtain ⅔ cup of juice.

Heat the sugar to a light caramel in a heavy saucepan over medium heat. Immediately add the vinegar and orange juice. Boil until all the caramel is dissolved. Add the duck stock and boil uncovered for 5 minutes, reducing the volume by one-quarter.

Blend the cornstarch with the water to make a thick paste and pour into the boiling sauce, stirring constantly with a whisk. Bring to a rolling boil and remove the pan from the heat.

Swirl in the butter; add the julienned rind, the orange liqueur, and salt and pepper to taste.

Monsieur François's hint to the home cook: When heating sugar to caramel without water, shake the pan often to prevent scorching.

Sauce de Canard aux Pommes

Apple Duck Sauce

Serves 4

1 tablespoon butter
1¼ cups finely diced apple, approximately 1 large apple
1½ cups duck stock (page 46)
1 tablespoon cornstarch
1 tablespoon water
¾ teaspoon salt
Large pinch of freshly ground pepper
2 teaspoons Calvados (apple brandy)

Melt the butter in a 1-quart saucepan. Add the diced apple and sauté for about 5 minutes, or until soft. Add 1 teaspoon of the Calvados and ignite. Then add the stock and bring to a boil. Reduce heat and simmer the sauce for about 15 minutes, reducing it by one-quarter.

In a cup, combine the cornstarch and cold water to make a paste. Pour this paste into the hot duck sauce, stirring constantly with a whisk to prevent lumps from forming. Bring to a boil again and simmer 2 or 3 minutes. Season with salt and pepper.

Remove from the heat and add the remaining Calvados. Taste and adjust seasonings.

Hollandaise Sauce

Pilfering is a significant factor in restaurant failure, and policing it a vital if unpleasant part of a chef's duties.

One morning during his pre-luncheon rounds, Papa spied Pierre, the *garde-manger*, scoop a large hunk of butter out of a tub, flatten it with a cleaver to facilitate concealment, and slip it between his apron and vest. Papa calmly summoned Pierre to the stove and without explanation directed him to make the hollandaise sauce. Pierre grimaced but said nothing as he began the assignment. He weighed the appropriate amount of butter, setting it in a pan to melt on the corner of the stove; separated the egg yolks into a copper bowl; and began cooking them in front of the hot oven. Papa stood back and watched for signs of discomfort.

After a few minutes, Pierre was clearly in distress. He began to sweat, occasionally glancing over his shoulder at his chef. As he continued to whisk the sauce, Pierre began to sway and later to hop from one leg to the other. By this time a noticeable butter stain had appeared on his apron just above the belt with a few streaks apparent down the leg of his checkered cook's pants. He had a baleful look. Papa fired him on the spot and called the *saucier* to incorporate the butter and yolks into a finished sauce.

Makes 3 cups

1 pound butter, clarified
5 egg yolks
2 tablespoons hot water
Juice of ½ lemon
1 teaspoon salt
Small pinch cayenne pepper

Melt the butter over low heat. Clarify by skimming off the foam and ladling out the butter, leaving the milky residue in the bottom of the pan.

In a copper or stainless steel bowl, whip together the 5 egg yolks and 2 tablespoons hot tap water with a whisk until smooth. Avoid aluminum as it discolors the yolks.

Cook over very low direct heat, or place the bowl over a pan of hot, but not boiling water. Beat continually, using the whisk to scrape the mixture from the bottom and sides of the bowl. Beating vigorously in a figure-8 pattern incorporates more air, and thereby produces a lighter sauce. (See the hint on page 50.)

To test for doneness, pull the whisk up out of the sauce; a thick ribbon rather than individual streams should form.

Remove from heat and slowly add the warm clarified butter, beating constantly. Should the sauce begin to separate, add 1 teaspoon cold water.

Season with the lemon juice, salt, and cayenne pepper to taste.

Strain the sauce through a fine sieve into a warm—not hot—stainless steel or nonmetallic bowl.

Béarnaise Sauce

This sauce, especially when made in a large quantity, requires a strong wrist and stamina. The end result, however, will make your effort worthwhile.

Makes 3 cups

½ teaspoon cracked black peppercorns (see hint on page 4)
1½ teaspoons shallots, chopped
1½ teaspoons tarragon leaves, chopped
1 tablespoon red wine vinegar
1 tablespoon tarragon wine vinegar
2 tablespoons dry white wine
5 egg yolks
2 tablespoons hot water
1 pound butter, clarified
Juice of ½ lemon
1 teaspoon salt
Small pinch of cayenne pepper
1 teaspoon parsley, chopped
1 teaspoon tarragon leaves, chopped

Combine the first six ingredients in a small saucepan and cook over medium heat until the liquid evaporates. Be careful not to scorch the reduction. Set aside.

In a copper or stainless steel bowl whip together with a whisk the 5 egg yolks and 2 tablespoons hot tap water until smooth. Avoid aluminum as it discolors the yolks.

Cook over very low direct heat or place bowl over a pan of hot, but not boiling, water. Beat continually, using the whisk to scrape the mixture from the bottom and sides of the bowl. Beating vigorously in a figure-8 pattern incorporates more air, and thereby produces a lighter sauce.

To test for doneness, pull the whisk up out of the sauce; a thick ribbon rather than individual streams should form.

Remove from the heat and slowly add the warm clarified butter, whipping constantly. Should sauce begin to separate, add 1 teaspoon cold water.

Whisk in the cooled reduction.

Season with lemon juice, salt, and cayenne pepper to taste.

Strain the sauce through a fine sieve into a warm—not hot—nonmetallic bowl. Mix in the finely chopped parsley and tarragon leaves.

Monsieur François's hints to the home cook: The egg yolks must be heated gradually over low heat to avoid scrambling them. The sauce must remain at a constant, tepid temperature or it will begin to separate. If the sauce cools, beat in a tablespoon of warm water. If the sauce curdles from overheating, beat in a tablespoon of cold water.

Beurre Blanc

White Butter Sauce

Makes 1 cup

½ pound (2 sticks) unsalted butter
½ cup dry white wine
2 tablespoons white wine vinegar
2 tablespoons finely minced shallots
⅛ teaspoon salt
Pinch of freshly ground pepper

Dice the butter and reserve in the refrigerator.

Combine the wine, vinegar, and shallots in a small saucepan and boil down, until almost dry. Reduce the heat to the lowest setting. Beat in the chilled butter, several pieces at a time. Whisk constantly until all the butter has been incorporated into the sauce and remove from heat. The sauce should have the consistency and appearance of a light hollandaise.

Taste and adjust seasonings. Transfer to a warm sauce boat and serve.

Monsieur François's hint to the home cook: Like Hollandaise and Béarnaise, white butter sauce may be prepared ahead and held if kept near body temperature.

Sauce Mayonnaise

Mayonnaise

Makes 1½ cups

2 egg yolks
1 teaspoon Dijon mustard
¼ teaspoon salt
1 teaspoon wine vinegar
1 teaspoon lemon juice
1 cup soya oil
Pinch of freshly ground white pepper

In a stainless steel or ceramic bowl, beat the egg yolks with a wire whisk.
Add the mustard, salt, vinegar, and lemon juice, and mix until well blended.

Add the oil by pouring in a slow steady stream and beating constantly.
If the sauce becomes too thick, thin it out with ½ teaspoon water.

Add the pepper and taste for seasoning.

Monsieur François's hint to the home cook: If time presses,
you can always buy a high quality mayonnaise. The object is to have
dinner, not satisfy an ideal.

Sauce Vincent

Herb Mayonnaise

Serves 4

1 cup mayonnaise (page 52)
1 tablespoon finely chopped watercress
3 tablespoons finely chopped parsley
1 hard-boiled egg, chopped
1 teaspoon Dijon mustard
1 teaspoon lemon juice
1 teaspoon finely minced onion
1 teaspoon finely chopped chives
1 tablespoon finely chopped fresh tarragon
½ teaspoon salt
Pinch of freshly ground black pepper
Pinch of cayenne pepper
1 teaspoon finely chopped capers

Place the mayonnaise in a small mixing bowl.

Put the parsley and watercress in a piece of clean cheesecloth, twist the ends together to close, and squeeze the juice from the herbs into the mayonnaise.

Add the remaining ingredients, including the watercress and parsley. Blend thoroughly. Taste and adjust the seasonings. Chill until ready to serve.

Monsieur François's hint to the home cook: At L'Auberge we have a large herb garden that supplies most of the fresh herbs used in this sauce. We do not make herb mayonnaise until the tarragon comes up in the spring.

Sauce Ravigote

Vinaigrette with Onions, Capers, and Gherkins

Serves 4

2 eggs, 1 raw and 1 hard-boiled and chopped
1 teaspoon prepared Dijon mustard, or ½ teaspoon dry mustard
⅓ cup tarragon wine vinegar
1 cup vegetable oil
1 teaspoon finely chopped onions
1 teaspoon finely chopped shallots
½ teaspoon finely chopped capers
½ teaspoon sour gherkins, finely chopped
1 teaspoon finely chopped parsley
1 teaspoon salt
¼ teaspoon freshly ground pepper
2 drops Tabasco sauce

In a mixing bowl, thoroughly beat the raw egg with a wire whisk. Add the mustard and vinegar and slowly pour in the oil, beating constantly. When all the oil is incorporated, blend in the remaining ingredients. Taste and correct the seasonings.

    Monsieur François's hint to the home cook: This sauce is also excellent with cold meats or used as a salad dressing.

Beurre d'Anchois

Anchovy Butter

Serves 4

½ pound unsalted butter
1½ ounces anchovy fillets
½ teaspoon lemon juice
¼ teaspoon finely minced shallots
1 teaspoon finely chopped parsley
Pinch of pepper

Soften the butter at room temperature for 1 hour.

Place the well-drained anchovy fillets in a food processor and purée. Add the remaining ingredients and blend thoroughly. Taste for seasonings, cover, and refrigerate.

Monsieur François's hint to the home cook: Serve the Anchovy Butter at room temperature.

Cranberry Sauce

Cranberry sauce is not French, you say! Well, no, but neither is my mother-in-law, Martha Harrison, at whose Thanksgiving table I so enjoyed her version of this all-American classic. At L'Auberge, we serve cranberry sauce with deer scallops, roast boar, and other game dishes.

Serves 8

1 pound fresh cranberries
1 medium orange
½ lemon
1 cup sugar

Remove the stems from the cranberries, wash, and drain well.

Quarter the orange. Remove the seeds and cut away the white membrane that runs down the center. Prepare the ½ lemon in the same manner.

Cut the orange and lemon half into several pieces. Place the pieces of fruit in a food processor, fitted with a steel blade and finely chop. Stop the machine and pour in the sugar and cranberries. Then purée all the ingredients together, just until they have a coarse consistency.

Pour into a bowl. Cover and chill overnight before serving.

Les Poissons

Fish

Truite au Bleu, Beurre Fondu

Poached Trout with Melted Butter

As an apprentice at L'Hôtel Chambard, Papa prepared literally thousands of *truite au bleu*. The *hôtel* had a large well in the courtyard that was stocked with trout from streams in the nearby Vosges Mountains.

When the chef called out the orders for trout, Papa ran to the well, netted the required number, and killed each with a hard blow on the head, using a section of an old broom stick. The trout were carefully gutted to avoid damaging the fillets, and the cavities were rinsed. To achieve a uniformly blue color, the trout must be handled as little as possible, sprinkled with vinegar and immediately plunged into a simmering *court bouillon*. The apprentice had to move fast and be ready to dash out again as the chef announced another *"truite au bleu"*!

Serves 4

2 quarts *court bouillon* (page 36)
4 fresh trout, 10 to 12 ounces each
⅓ cup red wine vinegar

Beurre fondue (butter sauce):
½ cup heavy cream
1½ sticks butter
Salt and freshly ground pepper to taste
½ tablespoon lemon juice

Prepare the *court bouillon* and have it simmering on the stove in a pan large enough to accommodate the four trout. Sprinkle the fish with the vinegar and slide them into the broth. Poach for 7 to 8 minutes after the broth returns to a boil.

Gently lift the trout from the broth and place on warm dinner plates. Serve garnished with lemon wedges, boiled potatoes, and *beurre fondue.*

To prepare the butter sauce, thicken the cream by boiling in a small saucepan for 2 to 3 minutes. Add the butter, cut into several pieces, shaking the pan until the butter has melted. Remove from the heat and add a pinch of salt and pepper. Blend in the lemon juice, swirl it all together, and serve.

Monsieur François's hint to the home cook: Substitute plain old melted butter for the above butter sauce.

Truites Farcies au Riesling d'Alsace

Stuffed Boneless Trout with Riesling Wine Sauce

Serves 4

Fish Mousse Stuffing:
½ pound trout, pike, or sole fillets
½ teaspoon salt
1 teaspoon freshly ground pepper
1 large egg
⅔ cup heavy whipping cream
½ teaspoon chopped truffles (optional)

Trout:
4 10 to 12-ounce trout
salt and freshly ground pepper
2 tablespoons butter
3 tablespoons finely chopped shallots
6 large white mushrooms
1½ cups Riesling wine

Sauce:
1 tablespoon butter
2 tablespoons flour
⅓ cup heavy whipping cream
4 to 5 drops lemon juice

Garnishes:
1 tablespoon butter
5 ounces Bay Scallops (½ cup)
½ tablespoon finely chopped shallots
salt and pepper
2 teaspoons finely chopped parsley

To prepare the stuffing, cut the fish fillets into one-inch pieces and place in a food processor fitted with a steel blade. Purée the fish until smooth, about one minute. With the processor running, add the egg, thoroughly blending it into the mousse. Add the salt and pepper and continue processing, while slowly pouring in the whipping cream. Stop the machine and scrape the mousse together. Add the truffles and give the mousse a final spin to blend all the ingredients thoroughly.

Refrigerate at least one hour.

Preheat the oven to 425 degrees.

To prepare the trout, place the previously gutted trout vertically in front of you. Beginning at either side, insert a sharp, thin knife between the fillet and ribs, just behind the head. Push the knife forward, keeping the blade flat against the ribs. Carefully separate the fillets from the ribs, down to the backbone on both sides, being careful not to cut through the skin along the back. Slide the blade under the central bone near the tail and cut it away from the fillets with a pair of heavy scissors.

Hold the tail in one hand and pull the bone toward the head with the other hand. Sever the spine with the scissors at the base of the head.

Lightly salt and pepper the trout cavities.

Place the mousse in a pastry bag fitted with a medium plain tube and beginning under the head, fill the trout cavities with the stuffing.

Butter the bottom of a medium roasting pan (approximately 12 by 14 inches) and sprinkle with the chopped shallots and a little salt and pepper. Clean and quarter the mushrooms and scatter them in the pan.

Carefully place the trout in the pan and pour in the white wine. Cover the trout with a piece of buttered wax paper or aluminum foil. Place the pan on the stove over high heat until the wine boils and transfer to the pre-heated oven. Bake for 12 to 14 minutes until the mousse is slightly firm to the touch. Remove the trout from the oven and reduce the temperature to the lowest setting. Carefully pour the liquid from the roasting pan into a small heavy saucepan.

Remove the fins and pull off the skin from the top side of each trout. Gently turn each one with the aid of a spatula, and remove the fin and skin from the other side. Replace the wax paper over the trout and return to the oven to keep warm (see hint page 71), along with four serving plates.

To prepare the sauce, place the saucepan containing the cooking liquid over high heat and prepare a *buerre manié* by thoroughly blending the softened butter and flour together with a fork. When the liquid boils, add the *beurre manié* and mix completely with a wire whisk. Reduce the heat and boil gently for 2 to 3 minutes. Pour in the heavy cream and bring to a boil once again. Reduce the heat to the lowest setting, add the lemon juice, and season to taste with salt and pepper. Keep warm.

To prepare the scallops, heat the one tablespoon of butter in a small skillet. When the butter begins to foam, add the scallops, shallots, and a little salt and pepper. Sauté for about one minute, tossing several times, and set aside.

To serve, remove the roasting pan and plates from the oven. Transfer one trout and ¼ of the mushrooms to each plate. Evenly divide the bay scallops around the trout. Pour any remaining pan juices into the sauce. Coat the trout with the sauce and sprinkle with the chopped parsley. Serve at once.

Monsieur François's hint to the home cook: You may substitute your favorite dry white wine in place of the Riesling.

Raie au Beurre Noir

Skatefish in Brown Butter
One of Monsieur François's personal favorites

Serves 4

2 quarts *court bouillon* (page 36)
4 pounds skate wings
2 teaspoons capers
1 stick butter
1 tablespoon vinegar

Prepare the *court bouillon* and have it simmering on the stove.

If the skate is purchased whole, separate the wings by cutting down the length of the fish on either side of the spine. Cut each wing into 2 to 3 large pieces and rinse under cold running water.

Poach the skate in the *court bouillon*. Begin timing the fish when the broth returns to a boil; pieces 1 inch thick will cook in approximately 10 minutes. Lift the skate out of the broth and place on a large platter or baking pan.

Warm four large dinner plates.

Using a fork, carefully scrape the dark skin off the top of the skate pieces. Slide the fork between the layer of bones that runs vertically through the wing. Lift off the top section of the fillet, keeping it as intact as possible. Remove the bones, flip the lower fillet over, and scrape off the skin.

Arrange the skate on the plates and sprinkle each portion with ½ teaspoon capers.

Melt the butter in a small saucepan over high heat until it turns dark brown, almost black, and pour over the skate. Add the vinegar to the hot pan, swirl around, and pour over the skate.

Serve with lemon wedges and boiled potatoes.

Shad Roe Sauté,
Beurre d'Anchois

Sautéed Shad Roe with Anchovy Butter

A sure sign of early spring is the arrival of shad in the local fish markets.

Serves 4

4 pairs medium shad roe
Salt and freshly ground black pepper
½ cup all-purpose flour
5 tablespoons butter
2 tablespoons vegetable oil

Season the roe lightly with salt and pepper. Dredge in the flour, brushing off the excess.

Heat half the butter and oil in each of two large sauté pans over a high flame until the butter browns. Add the shad roe and cook for 4 to 5 minutes per side. Overcooking dries out the roe.

Transfer to warm plates. Serve with lemon wedges and anchovy butter (page 55).

Monsieur François's hint to the home cook: The actual cooking time depends on size, thickness, cooking temperature, etc. The roe is done when slightly firm and springy to the touch.

Sea Squabs Sauteed
with Red and Green Peppers

Sea Squabs Sautéed with Red and Green Peppers

Sea squabs are North Atlantic blowfish. They are very meaty, have no bones other than the spine, and are sold skinned with the heads removed.

Serves 2

2 small bell peppers, 1 green and 1 red
½ pounds fresh mushrooms, cleaned and quartered
4 tablespoons butter
4 to 6 sea squabs per person (approximately ½ pound per serving)
Salt and freshly ground pepper
All-purpose flour
1 tablespoon oil
1 tablespoon lemon juice
½ stick butter for brown butter

Preheat oven to 450 degrees.

Brush both the peppers with a little oil, place in a small pan and bake until their skins turn dark brown, approximately 5 to 8 minutes. Cool until they can be handled easily, and then rub off the skin. Split the peppers in half lengthwise, cut off the stems, discard the seeds and white membranes. Dice and set aside.

Reduce the oven to 400 degrees.

Sauté the mushrooms in 2 tablespoons of the butter over high heat for 2 to 3 minutes until soft. Add the diced peppers, tossing once or twice. Remove from heat, season with salt and pepper and reserve.

Season the sea squabs with salt and pepper and dredge in the flour, shaking off the excess. Heat 2 tablespoons of the butter and the oil in a large skillet. When the butter begins to brown, add the sea squabs and sauté for 1 to 2 minutes until lightly browned. Turn the fish over and set the pan in the oven for about 5 minutes.

Remove the pan from the oven and place equal portions of the fish on two ovenproof plates. Carefully pull off the central fin from each of the sea squabs. Sprinkle with the lemon juice. Scatter the mushrooms and peppers around the fish. Put the plates in the oven for 2 to 3 minutes to heat.

Melt ½ stick of butter until it turns a light brown and pour over the fish as they come out of the oven.

Serve with *tomates provençale* (page 157).

Monsieur François's hint to the home cook: To remove excess flour, place the sea squabs in a large sieve and shake it back and forth. Use this method for shrimp, scallops, or any small pieces of meat or fish.

*Le Saumon Soufflé
de l'Auberge*

Salmon Soufflé

I was very fortunate to have spent several weeks at the three-star L'Auberge de L'Ill in Alsace, France, with Master Chef Paul Haeberlin. This is our version of his original dish.

Serves 8

Pike mousse:
1 pound pike fillets (sea bass may be substituted)
3 whole medium eggs
¾ teaspoon salt
¼ teaspoon freshly ground pepper
1¾ cups heavy whipping cream
1 teaspoon freshly chopped truffles (optional)

Salmon:
4 tablespoons butter
Salt and pepper
2 tablespoons chopped shallots
2 pounds salmon fillets
2 cups dry white wine

Sauce:
1½ cups *sauce Américaine* (page 38)
½ cup heavy whipping cream
2 tablespoons butter
1 tablespoon cognac
1 teaspoon sherry
Salt and pepper to taste

Garnish:
Meat from a 1- to 2-pound steamed lobster
16 large *champignons à blanc* (page 160)
⅓ cup *tomates concassés* (page 158)

To prepare the mousse, cut the pike into 1-inch pieces and force through the fine disc of a meat grinder. (You may omit this step without appreciably changing the result if a grinder is unavailable.) Purée the fish in a food processor fitted with a steel blade.

Add the eggs, one at a time, thoroughly blending each into the mousse. Add the salt and pepper. With the processor running, pour in the heavy cream, ¼ cup at a time. until completely incorporated. Add the chopped truffle and give the mousse a final spin. Remove from the processor and refrigerate at least one hour.

Preheat the oven to 400 degrees.

To prepare the salmon, butter a small baking pan, and sprinkle it with salt and pepper and the chopped shallots.

64

Cut the salmon into eight equal portions and lightly salt and pepper. With the aid of a small spatula, cover each slice with the pike mousse, forming a dome. Place the covered salmon fillets in the pan and add the white wine. Bring to a full boil on the stove. Transfer the pan to the oven and bake until the mousse begins to firm, 12 to 15 minutes. While the salmon is cooking, heat the sauce and prepare the garnishes.

Boil the sauce with the cream and reduce the heat. Beat in the butter, cognac, and sherry with a whisk. Taste for seasoning. Keep warm.

Cut the steamed lobster tail into rounds ½-inch thick and split the claw meat in half, lengthwise.

Cook the mushrooms caps and keep warm.

Heat the *tomates concassées*.

Remove the salmon from the oven and set the oven control to broil. Place the soufflé on an ovenproof plate. Garnish with lobster meat and two inverted mushroom caps filled with the *tomates concassées*. Lightly brown the soufflés under the broiler. Pour the warm sauce around the plate and serve at once.

Médaillons de Lotte et Pétoncles au Champagne

Monkfish and Bay Scallops in Champagne Sauce

Virtually unknown in the United States until recently, *lotte* (anglerfish) is a favorite fish in France. Also called "poor man's lobster" and monkfish, it has a large ugly head and dark robe-like skin.

Serves 4

2½ pounds monkfish
6 tablespoons butter
1 tablespoon minced shallots
2 cups sliced raw mushrooms, approximately ⅔ pound
Salt and pepper
1 cup champagne
⅓ pound bay scallops
1 teaspoon lemon juice
1¼ cups heavy whipping cream
1 teaspoon finely chopped parsley

Separate the 2 lobed fillets of the fish by removing the large spinal column. Remove the dark outer skin and translucent gray inner skin, exposing the white flesh. Slice the fillets into ¼-inch rounds or medallions.

Preheat oven to 400 degrees.

Smear 2 tablespoons of the butter and the shallots in a small (9-by-13-inch) baking pan. Lay the medallions in the pan in a single layer and cover with the sliced mushrooms. Season with salt and pepper and pour the champagne over the fish. Place the pan over direct heat until the wine begins to boil. Cover the pan with a lid or sheet of aluminum foil and set in the oven for 5 minutes.

While the fish is baking, melt another 2 tablespoons of the butter in a small saucepan over medium heat. Add the scallops and sprinkle with the lemon juice and salt and pepper. Simmer in the butter for 1 to 2 minutes, shaking the pan often until the scallops turn white. Lift the scallops from the pan with a slotted spoon and set aside.

Remove the baking pan containing the monkfish from the oven and pour the juices into the saucepan just used for the scallops. Place the scallops in the baking pan with the monkfish, and replace the cover to keep the fish warm. Reduce the liquid in the saucepan over high heat until it has almost completely evaporated. Add the cream and boil 3 to 4 minutes, until it is thick enough to coat a spoon. Remove the pan from the heat and beat in the last 2 tablespoons of butter with a whisk. Season with salt and pepper.

Divide the fish, mushrooms, and scallops among the four dinner plates and set in the oven a few moments to heat. Spoon the sauce over the monkfish, garnish with the parsley, and serve.

Monsieur François's hint to the home cook: Monkfish becomes very tough if overcooked. See the hint on page 70.

Baked Sea Bass in Sorrel Sauce

Serves 4

1 cup fresh sorrel leaves
1 quart water
1 tablespoon salt
1 3- to 4-pound sea bass, filleted and skinned
2 tablespoons butter
1 tablespoon finely minced shallots
½ pound white mushrooms, washed and sliced
Salt and freshly ground pepper
1 cup dry white wine

Sorrel sauce:
Cooking liquids from the pan of fish
1¼ cups heavy cream
Sorrel purée
3 tablespoons hollandaise sauce (page 49)
½ teaspoon salt
Pinch of pepper

Remove the stems and any discolored leaves from the sorrel. Parboil the sorrel leaves in the quart of salted boiling water for 1 or 2 minutes. Drain well and purée in a blender or food processor.

Preheat oven to 400 degrees.

Cut the two bass fillets in half. Butter a flameproof baking pan and scatter the chopped shallots over the bottom. Place bass fillets in the pan and cover with the sliced mushrooms. Sprinkle with salt and freshly ground pepper.

Pour the white wine around the fish fillets and bring to a boil over high heat. Cover the pan with a tight-fitting lid or a piece of aluminum foil. Transfer to the preheated oven and cook for 7 to 8 minutes. Remove the pan from the oven and proceed with the sorrel sauce.

To make the sauce, pour the liquid from the pan of baked fish into a small saucepan. Place the cover back over the fish, set aside, and keep warm. Bring the liquid to a boil and reduce by three-quarters. Add the heavy cream and boil gently for 5 minutes. Stir in the sorrel purée and remove from the heat. With a whisk, blend in the 3 tablespoons of hollandaise sauce. Add the salt and pepper to taste.

Place the fish, topped with the mushrooms, on warm plates and cover with the sauce. Serve at once.

Monsieur François's hint to the home cook: Serve the remaining hollandaise with steamed asparagus or broccoli as an accompaniment to the bass. See also the hint on page 70.

Steak d'Espadon sauté aux Cinq Poivres

Sautéed Swordfish with Combination Peppercorns

Serves 2

2 8-ounce center cut swordfish steaks (¾- to 1-inch thick)
salt
2 level teaspoons coarsely ground *cinq poivres* (see hint below)
2 tablespoons butter
1 tablespoon vegetable oil
Sautéed wild mushrooms, sautéed sugar snap peas (page 151)
Béarnaise sauce (page 50)

Salt the swordfish steaks and gently press ½ teaspoon of the ground peppercorn mixture into each side.

Heat the butter and oil in a 12-inch skillet. When the butter begins to brown, add the steaks and sear over a high heat. Cook for approximately 2 to 3 minutes. Do not overcook.

Serve on warm plates with the sautéed wild mushrooms, sugar snap peas, and the Béarnaise sauce.

Monsieur François's hint to the home cook: *cinq poivres*, a five peppercorn combination of black, white, red and green peppers, packaged in France, is found in gourmet shops. You may substitute coarsely ground black peppercorns (page 4). However, use only ¼ to ⅓ teaspoon of the stronger black pepper, per side.

Loup de Mer et Julienne de Céleri Rave

Rockfish with Celery Root Julienne

Serves 4

Celery root (celeriac):
2 large celery roots (must yield 2 cups celery root, julienne)
2 tablespoons butter
Salt and pepper

Fish:
2 tablespoons butter
1 tablespoon finely minced shallots
2 3- to 4-pound rockfish, filleted and skinned
Salt and pepper
1 cup dry white wine
1 recipe for *beurre blanc* seasoned with 1 tablespoon minced chives
  (page 51)

Peel the celery root and slice into medium julienne strips. Cover with a damp towel and set aside.

Preheat oven to 400 degrees.

Butter a 9-by-13-inch baking pan with 2 tablespoons of butter. Sprinkle the bottom of the pan with the shallots. Lay the fillets on top, season with salt and pepper, and add the wine. Place on top of the stove over a high heat until the wine boils.

Cover the pan with aluminum foil and bake in the oven for 8 to 10 minutes.

While the fish is baking, prepare the celery root. Melt 2 tablespoons of butter in a medium saucepan. When the foam subsides, add the celery root, and sauté for 2 to 3 minutes. Season with salt and pepper.

When the fish is done, transfer it onto warm plates with a slotted spatula. Scatter the celery root on top and ladle the warm *beurre blanc* around the fish. Serve at once.

Monsieur François's hint to the home cook: Substitute parboiled julienned fennel bulb for the celeriac.

Filets de Sole aux Nouilles

Fillets of Sole with Noodles

Serves 4

12 fillets of lemon or grey sole (approximately 2 pounds)
Salt and freshly ground pepper
4 tablespoons butter
2 tablespoons shallots, finely minced
⅓ cup hollandaise sauce (page 49)
1 cup heavy whipping cream
6 to 8 ounces noodles
¾ cup dry white wine
¾ cup fish stock (page 37)
Pinch of grated nutmeg

Season the fillets with salt and pepper and fold each in half, lengthwise. Butter a flameproof casserole with 2 tablespoons of the butter and sprinkle with the shallots. Place the sole fillets in the casserole and reserve in the refrigerator.

Make the hollandaise sauce.

Whip half the heavy whipping cream and reserve.

Preheat the broiler.

Cook the noodles in boiling salted water until *al dente*. Drain and reserve.

Cover the fish fillets with the white wine and fish stock. Bring to a boil over high heat. Reduce the heat and cover. Simmer gently for 5 minutes, or until the fish are cooked. Remove from the heat. Strain the poaching liquid into a heavy saucepan. Bring to a boil and reduce by three-quarters.

In another saucepan, bring ½ cup of the heavy cream to a boil. Reduce for 2 minutes, add a pinch of salt, pepper, and the grated nutmeg. Lower the heat and blend in the remaining 2 tablespoons of butter with a whisk. Stir in the noodles and gently heat for a few moments.

When poaching liquid is reduced, remove it from the heat and allow to cool slightly. Gently fold in the hollandaise and the whipped cream. Taste for seasoning and adjust if necessary.

Place equal portions of the noodles onto four ovenproof plates. Arrange three fillets per plate on top of the noodles and coat with the sauce. Brown lightly under the broiler and serve immediately.

May be served with broccoli or asparagus hollandaise.

Monsieur François's hint to the home cook: Assigning a specific cooking time for fish is very difficult. Fish is done when slightly firm and springy to the touch. Another test is to place a knife or narrow spatula under the fillet and lift it to expose the center. Remove the fish just as the center turns from translucent to opaque.

Paupriettes de Sole aux Huitres

Fillets of Sole with Julienned Vegetables and Oysters

Serves 4

⅓ cup each, julienned leeks, carrots, and celery root
12 individual fillets of sole (lemon or grey sole), deboned and skinned
Salt and pepper
4 tablespoons butter
2 tablespoons minced shallots
1½ cups fish stock (page 37)
1 cup dry white wine
20 shucked medium-sized oysters
½ cup heavy cream
Freshly chopped parsley

Cut the vegetables into matchstick-size julienne pieces and parboil in salted water for 2 minutes. Immediately plunge into cold water, drain, and reserve.

Lay the sole fillets, white side down, on your work surface. Season lightly with salt and pepper. Divide the vegetables into 12 portions and place each bundle on the large end of a fillet. Fold the end of the sole fillet over the vegetables in jelly-roll fashion. Place them folded side down in a small baking pan smeared with 2 tablespoons of the butter and the minced shallots. Pour 1 cup of the fish stock and 1 cup white wine over the fish. Place over a high flame, cover, and boil for 5 minutes. Remove from the heat and set aside.

Bring the remaining ½ cup fish stock to a boil and drop in the oysters. Lift the oysters out of the stock with a slotted spoon as soon as the stock begins to boil again, and set them aside.

Drain the liquid from the pan of cooked sole into the oyster broth. Boil over high heat until reduced by three-quarters. Add the cream, boil 1 to 2 minutes, and then remove from the heat. With a whisk, blend in the remaining 2 tablespoons of butter and adjust seasonings.

Divide the oysters and sole onto four warm plates. Coat with the sauce and sprinkle with the chopped parsley.

Monsieur François's hint to the home cook: Keep the fish warm while preparing the sauce by leaving a small amount of the cooking liquid in the bottom of the pan and covering the fish with a damp towel. Set the pan in a 200-degree oven or leave the door open if the oven is hot. The fish will remain warm and moist without overcooking for about 15 minutes.

Red Snapper à la Duxelles

Red Snapper with Mushroom Purée

During the first year, apprentices spend much of their time cleaning. One morning, *le patron* announced that one of his huge wine casks was empty and needed a thorough scrubbing. The opening was narrow, so Papa, the youngest and smallest, was selected for the job. The lid was removed, releasing powerful wine fumes. Papa was then lowered into the cask to wash down the sides and flush out the dregs.

After awhile, the chef went down to *la cave* to scold Papa for taking such a long time—an apprentice must learn to work quickly! As the chef entered the cellar, he heard muffled singing. He could hardly believe his ears! Imagine, an apprentice singing on the job. Unthinkable! Climbing up the ladder, he barked at François to come out instantly. Poor Papa, however, could not negotiate the narrow passage, having been intoxicated by the wine fumes. He was rescued by the *sommelier* and sent straight to bed to sleep it off.

Serves 4

1 cup *duxelles* (page 159)
1 cup hollandaise sauce (page 49)
1 cup heavy cream, whipped
2 tablespoons butter
1 tablespoon finely minced shallots
4 8- to 10-ounce red snapper fillets
Salt and pepper to taste
1 cup dry white wine
¼ teaspoon freshly squeezed lemon juice

Prepare the *duxelles* and hollandaise sauce.

Whip the heavy cream and refrigerate.

Preheat oven to 400 degrees.

Butter a small baking pan and sprinkle with the shallots. Lay the snapper fillets on the shallots and season with salt and pepper. Pour the wine around the fish, place the pan on the stove over high heat, and bring to a boil. Cover the pan with a lid or a sheet of aluminum foil, transfer to the oven, and bake 8 to 10 minutes.

When the fillets are done, remove them from the pan and place on a serving platter. Coat the fish with the mushroom purée, cover with the foil, and keep warm. Set oven to broil.

Pour the pan juices into a small saucepan and reduce over high heat until almost dry. Remove the pan from the heat and cool slightly for a minute or two. Add the whipped cream and then the hollandaise sauce and lemon juice, blending carefully. Taste and adjust seasonings. Coat the snapper fillets with the sauce and brown lightly under the broiler. Serve immediately.

Red Snapper
dans sa Robe Croustillante

Red Snapper in Puff Pastry

Serves 2

2 rounded tablespoons lump crab meat
2 rounded tablespoons *duxelles* (page 159)
12 to 14 ounces puff pastry (page 167)
1 10- to 12-ounce red snapper fillet
salt and freshly ground pepper
1 egg, beaten
½ medium green or red bell pepper
4 heaping tablespoons pike mousse (page 64)

Garnishes:
glazed carrots and onions (page 150)
baked tomatoes with herbs (page 157)
sautéed sugar snap peas (page 151)
lemon wedges
Buerre blanc (page 51)

Prepare the pike mousse and *duxelles*, chilling both thoroughly.

Slice the pepper into ¼ inch thick strips and blanch for 1 minute. Drain thoroughly and chill. Roll the puff pastry on a floured surface into a rectangle, approximately 12 by 14 by ⅛ inches. Cut the dough in half lengthwise to obtain two 6 by 14 inch rectangles. Brush off any excess flour and place one of the rectangles on an ungreased cookie sheet.

Salt and pepper the red snapper fillet and center it on the dough. Spread the *duxelles* evenly over the fillet. Place the pepper strips and the crab meat down the center of the fish.

Mound the mousse over the crab meat. (Any *duxelles*, crab meat, or mousse that falls onto the dough must be removed and piled back on the fillet, or the two layers of dough will not adhere properly.)

Brush the dough around the fillet with the egg wash. Lift and center the second layer of puff pastry on top of the mousse. Press the two layers of dough together with the sides of your hands.

Shape and decorate the dough into a fish form as follows: Place the encased red snapper vertically in front of you. With a small knife, fashion one large fin on the upper left hand side and two small fins on the lower right hand side. Shape a tail at the bottom and trim the remaining dough along the sides to a point at the top, completing the fish form.

The dough trimmings may be used to further embellish the "fish." Cut into strips to adorn the head or roll into a ball, as an eye. (The egg wash is used as a glue to adhere the decorations.) The scales are sculpted by pushing the small end of a pastry tube halfway through the dough and pulling back slightly. (Any markings must be actually cut into the dough.

Those merely pressed in the dough will not be visible after baking.)

Refrigerate the fish for at least 2 hours before baking.

Preheat the oven to 375 degrees.

Prepare the vegetable garnishes.

Brush the fish with the egg wash and bake for approximately 35 minutes, until golden brown. (If the fish browns too quickly, lower the heat and cover with foil.) While the fish is baking, prepare the *beurre blanc*.

Just before removing the fish from the oven, arrange the vegetable garnishes around the edges of a large serving tray. Place the tray in the oven for 4 to 5 minutes to heat the vegetables. Transfer the fish to the serving tray with the aid of a large spatula and present in the dining room.

Cut the fish in two and at tableside, serve on warm plates with the garnishes and sauce.

Monsieur François's hint to the home cook: Substitute a salmon or sea bass in place of the red snapper. Use a thick fillet, as a thin one will dry out before the dough is cooked. The amount of mousse required for one fish is less than ¼ recipe (page 64). Since it is difficult to make less than ½ recipe, I suggest making several red snappers in puff pastry or using the extra fish mousse to prepare a small fish paté. (See page 29).

Choucroute de Poissons Fumés

Seafood Sauerkraut

A modern rendition of the Alsatian classic featuring smoked fish.

Serves 4

4 pounds sauerkraut
2 tablespoons butter
1 cup slivered onions
½ teaspoon salt
2½ cups dry white wine
1 *bouquet garni* consisting of 1 bay leaf, 2 cloves, 2 cloves garlic crushed,
    ¼ teaspoon thyme, 10 crushed juniper berries, and 8 cracked black
    peppercorns (see hint on page 4), wrapped in cheesecloth
12 small potatoes
¾ pound smoked salmon
¾ pound smoked whitefish
¾ pound smoked sturgeon
¾ pound smoked finnan haddie
1 quart water
2 cups milk
½ pound sea scallops
Beurre blanc (page 51)

Preheat oven to 350 degrees.

Place the sauerkraut in a colander and rinse with cold water. Press the sauerkraut with your hands to remove as much moisture as possible.

Melt the butter in a heavy saucepan and simmer the onions until limp, but do not brown. Add the sauerkraut, salt, wine, and *bouquet garni* and bring to a boil. Cover, transfer to the oven, and cook for 1½ hours. The sauerkraut should remain somewhat crisp.

While the sauerkraut is cooking, boil the potatoes in a pot of salted water for 20 to 25 minutes, or until tender. Peel and keep warm.

Skin and remove any small bones from the smoked fish. Cut the fish fillets into four portions.

Combine the quart of water and two cups of milk in a large shallow saucepan. Bring to a boil; then reduce heat so the liquid just simmers. Add the smoked fish 20 minutes before serving. Add the scallops 5 minutes before serving.

Remove the sauerkraut from the oven and adjust the seasonings. Mound the sauerkraut on a large oval or rectangular platter. Lift the fish and scallops out of the liquid with a slotted spoon and arrange around the sauerkraut along with the potatoes.

Serve immediately with *beurre blanc*.

Monsieur François's hint to the home cook: Smoked tuna, shrimp and scallops are sometimes to be found in fancy food stores and may be used with or in place of the other fish.

Saumon Froid, Sauce Vincent

Cold Salmon with Green Herb Mayonnaise

Serves 4

1 quart *court bouillon* (page 36)
2 tablespoons butter
1 teaspoon minced shallots
Salt and freshly ground pepper
1½ pounds salmon fillet, deboned but not skinned
Sauce Vincent (page 53)

Prepare the *court bouillon*.

Generously butter an 8-by-10-inch baking pan and sprinkle with the minced shallots, salt, and pepper. Slice the fillet into four pieces and place skin side down in the pan.

Pour the hot *court bouillon* over the salmon. The slices should be completely submerged in the broth.

Place the pan on top of the stove over high heat and bring to a boil. Reduce the heat. Cover the pan with a lid or a piece of heavy aluminum foil and simmer gently for approximately 10 minutes. (The rule is to measure the fish at its thickest point and allow 10 minutes per inch.)

Remove the pan from the stove and let the fish cool in the broth.

Refrigerate until time to serve.

Remove the servings of fish from the chilled broth, peel off the skin, and place on the serving dish. Coat with Sauce Vincent. Serve with hard-boiled eggs, tomato wedges, and fresh green salad.

Monsieur François's hint to the home cook: Prepare the salmon the day before to ensure that it is completely cold before serving.

Les Coquillages et Crustacés

Shellfish

Noix de Coquilles St. Jacques,
Echalotes, ail et tomates

Sautéed Scallops, Mediterranean Style

As an apprentice in France, Papa was required to prepare the staff's meals. On one occasion a waitress complained to the chef that the food was too salty. Enraged, the chef punched the 16-year-old François in the mouth, breaking his right front tooth. The moral is: Always taste before adding salt. The amount of salt indicated in these recipes is only a guideline; please use your own judgment.

For those dining at L'Auberge, many dishes can be prepared sans salt. It is simply a matter of stating your preference to your waiter or waitress.

Serves 2

¾ pound fresh sea scallops
½ cup quartered mushrooms
½ stick butter
2 tablespoons olive oil
½ teaspoon salt
Pinch of freshly ground pepper
¼ cup flour
1 tablespoon minced shallots
½ cup diced cooked tomatoes
1 teaspoon minced fresh garlic
1 tablespoon lemon juice
½ teaspoon chopped parsley

Cut any large scallops in half, horizontally. Rinse the scallops under cold water and drain well in a colander.

Clean and quarter the mushrooms. Heat 1 tablespoon of the butter and 1 tablespoon of the oil in a large skillet over high heat. Sauté the mushrooms for 3 or 4 minutes and season with salt and pepper. Transfer the mushrooms into a small bowl and reserve. Wipe the pan clean.

Season the scallops with salt and pepper and dredge in flour. Remove excess flour by shaking the scallops back and forth in a sieve.

Heat the remaining butter and oil over high heat. When the butter begins to brown, add the scallops in a single layer. Brown the scallops on one side for 2 minutes, turn with a pair of tongs, and brown the other side for 2 minutes.

Scatter the shallots over the scallops and toss once or twice. Add the tomatoes, garlic, lemon juice, and quartered mushrooms. (Drain the mushrooms if any juice has accumulated in the bowl.) Toss several times until all are evenly distributed.

Transfer the scallops to warm plates and sprinkle with the chopped parsley. Serve with lemon wedges and *tomates provençale* (page 157).

Monsieur François's finishing touch: Prepare this dish using half scallops and half raw, peeled shrimp, and serve with a small amount of Madeira sauce (page 40).

Soft-Shell-Crabs
Amandine

Soft-Shell Crabs with Almonds

Serves 4

Beer batter:
2 eggs
½ cup flour
½ cup beer
½ teaspoon salt
¼ teaspoon freshly ground pepper

Crabs:
1 cup slivered almonds
8 large soft-shelled crabs
6 tablespoons plus 1 stick butter
2 tablespoons oil

Prepare the batter at least one-half hour before use.

Beat the eggs in a large bowl with a wire whisk. Blend in the flour until smooth. Slowly pour in the beer, beating the mixture until any lumps are dissolved. Season with salt and pepper. Set aside.

Heat oven to 400 degrees.

Spread the almonds in a single layer on a baking sheet and toast in the oven until lightly browned.

Use only live crabs. To prepare them, cut away the pointed apron, the eyes, and face of each crab with a pair of heavy shears. Lift the long points on each side of the back shell and remove the spongy gills. Wash the crabs by dipping them in a bowl of cold water.

Use two large skillets to sauté the crabs; cook four in each.

Heat 3 tablespoons butter and 1 tablespoon oil in one of the skillets over high heat. As the butter begins to brown, rapidly dip each crab in the batter for an instant, lift to drain off excess batter, then place upside down in the hot butter. As the last crab is placed in the pan, the first crab will probably be browned enough to flip over. When all the crabs are nicely browned and turned over, transfer the pan to the 400-degree oven. Repeat the process with the remaining four crabs. Bake the crabs for 5 minutes— do not overcook. Place two crabs on each of four warmed plates.

Wipe out one of the skillets, place over high heat, and melt the stick of butter. When the butter has browned, add the toasted almonds and toss once or twice. Spoon the butter and almonds over the crabs and serve with lemon wedges and *tomates provençale* (page 157).

Monsieur François's hint to the home cook: Beware of so-called "paper skin"—partially soft crabs which are often too tough to eat. The crabs may be merely dredged in flour and sautéed, rather than dipped in the batter.

Soupière de Crustacés des Gourmands

Our Shellfish Bouillabaisse

My father's version of bouillabaisse featuring shellfish and julienned vegetables.

Serves 6

⅓ cup olive oil
½ cup finely chopped onion
½ cup finely julienned leeks
¼ cup finely julienned celery
½ cup finely julienned carrots
1 tablespoon minced shallots
1½ cups chopped fresh tomatoes
½ cup tomato paste
1 cup dry white wine
3 cups fish stock (page 37)
2 tablespoons salt
1 *bouquet garni* consisting of 1 teaspoon fennel seed,
    1 teaspoon anise seed, 1 teaspoon cracked black peppercorns
    (see hint on page 4), 2 bay leaves, 3 cloves, pinch of thyme
    and 2 cloves garlic crushed, wrapped in a cheesecloth
½ teaspoon saffron
30 mussels
18 little neck clams
1 pound sea scallops
3 1-pound Maine lobsters
1 pound raw shrimp (20-24 count)
2 pounds fish fillets (red snapper, sea bass, or swordfish)
1 stick butter
1 tablespoon finely chopped garlic
1 loaf French bread
1 tablespoon Pernod
1 tablespoon finely chopped fresh fennel
3 tablespoons chopped parsley

Heat the olive oil in a large saucepan or Dutch oven. Add the onions, leeks, celery, and carrots and cook covered until tender, about 15 minutes, stirring often.

Add the shallots, tomatoes, tomato paste, 1 cup white wine, 3 cups fish stock, salt, and *bouquet garni*. Boil for approximately 25 minutes.

Add the saffron, and simmer 5 more minutes.

While the broth is cooking, prepare the seafood.

Clean the mussels individually under cold running water, scraping off any clinging barnacles or "beards." Discard any half-open shells or any unusually heavy ones, indicating internal grit.

Rinse the clams and scallops in cold water.

Using a sharp heavy knife, force the point of the blade through the top of the lobster head between the eyes; then cut down through the center of the head and tail, splitting the lobster in half. Remove and discard the stomach sac behind the eyes, and the intestinal vein running down the center of the tail. Remove the claws and crack them with the blunt edge of the blade.

Peel and devein the shrimp.

Cut the fish fillets into 2- to 3-inch diagonal slices.

Melt the butter and garlic together. Cut the loaf of bread into slices ¼-inch thick. Brush both sides with the garlic butter and toast under the broiler.

To prepare the soupière, add the mussels and clams to the boiling broth and simmer 5 minutes. Then add the lobster, shrimp, scallops, and fish. Continue boiling until all the shellfish are open, approximately 5 to 8 more minutes. Do not overcook.

Remove from heat, adjust seasoning (more garlic or saffron according to taste), add Pernod, chopped fennel, and parsley, and serve immediately in large warm soup platters.

Garnish with the garlic toasts.

Monsieur François's hint to the home cook: Prepare the broth ahead and refrigerate. Reheat and cook the seafood just prior to serving.

Queues de Langoustes
et Crevettes Chez François

Lobster Tails and Shrimp with Herb and Garlic Butter

Serves 4

Herb butter:
1 pound lightly salted butter
2 tablespoons chopped parsley
1 tablespoon lemon juice
Drop of Tabasco sauce
1 teaspoon Worcestershire sauce
½ teaspoon each, finely ground anise seed and fennel seed
½ teaspoon ground pepper
¾ teaspoon salt
1 tablespoon finely minced shallots
1 heaping tablespoon finely chopped garlic
¼ cup dry white wine

Shellfish:
1 pound raw shrimp (16–20 count)
4 8-ounce lobster tails
2 tablespoons lightly salted butter
1 cup dry white wine

Begin by preparing the herb butter.

Soften the butter at room temperature for 1 hour. Whip the butter and all the other ingredients together with an electric mixer or food processor. Cover and refrigerate until time to use.

Peel and devein the shrimp. (Reserve the shells in the freezer for shrimp bisque, page 12.) Cut the lobster tails into rounds ½ to ¾ inch thick with a small cleaver.

Preheat oven to 400 degrees.

Butter a flameproof baking dish with the 2 tablespoons of butter and arrange the shrimp and lobster tails in the pan. Add the white wine, place over direct heat and bring to a boil. Cover the pan and bake in the oven for 5 minutes, just until the lobsters begin to turn white. Be sure not to overcook.

Set the oven to broil.

Lift the seafood from the pan and divide evenly between four oven-proof plates.

Dot the shrimp and lobster tails with 3 tablespoons of herb butter per serving. Place under the broiler until the butter melts and serve at once.

Serve with wilted spinach, page 146.

Monsieur François's hint to the home cook: Use the same herb butter to prepare snails.

*Homard grillé
farci au Crabe*

Broiled Lobster Stuffed with Crabmeat

Serves 2

2 1½ pound live Maine lobsters
Salt and pepper
½ teaspoon mild paprika
¾ cup (1½ sticks) plus 2 tablespoons butter
2 teaspoons lemon juice
½ pound lump crabmeat
1 teaspoon finely minced shallots
½ teaspoon lemon juice
½ teaspoon chopped parsley

Preheat broiler.

Using a sharp heavy knife, force the point of the blade through the top of the lobster head between the eyes; then cut down and through the center of the head and tail, splitting the lobster in two. Remove and discard the stomach sac behind the eyes and the intestinal vein in the center of the tail. Remove the claws and crack them with the blunt side of the knife blade.

Place the split lobsters in a shallow baking pan, lightly salt and pepper them, and dust with paprika. Dot each lobster half with ¼ stick butter and sprinkle with ½ teaspoon lemon juice.

Place under broiler for 5 minutes, then reduce heat to 425 degrees and finish cooking the lobsters in the oven for approximately 5 more minutes; this method prevents the delicate meat from drying out.

While the lobster is cooking, carefully remove any pieces of shell from the crabmeat, retaining as many large lumps as possible. Melt the 2 tablespoons of butter in a small sauté pan. When the butter begins to brown, add the shallots, cook a few seconds, and then add the crabmeat and a pinch of salt and pepper. Toss gently and add the lemon juice and chopped parsley. Set aside. Wipe out pan and brown the remaining ½ stick of butter.

Remove lobsters from oven and place on two warm plates. With the aid of a rubber spatula, pour the pan juice over the lobsters. Portion the crabmeat into the lobster halves. Serve with the brown butter and lemon wedges.

Monsieur François's hint to the home cook: The lobster will be most appreciated even without the crabmeat.

Mousseline de Crabe
et Écrevisses Marie-Antoinette

Mousseline of Crab and Crayfish

Serves 6

2 quarts *court bouillon* (page 36)
50 live crayfish, approximately 5 pounds

Bisque d'écrevisses (crayfish sauce):
¼ cup olive oil
½ cup finely chopped onions
⅓ cup finely chopped carrots
⅓ cup finely chopped leeks
2 tablespoons finely chopped celery
1 tablespoon finely minced shallots
Reserved crayfish heads and tails
⅓ cup sherry
1 cup dry white wine
2 cups reserved *court bouillon*
3 tablespoons tomato purée
1 bay leaf
2 cloves
¼ teaspoon thyme
¼ teaspoon tarragon
¼ teaspoon freshly ground pepper
1 clove garlic, crushed
Beurre manié consisting of 2 teaspoons softened butter and
    2 teaspoons all-purpose flour
1 teaspoon butter
⅓ cup heavy whipping cream
1 teaspoon cognac

Molds:
1 recipe pike mousse (page 64)
2 tablespoons butter
2 tablespoons finely minced shallots
½ cup shredded Bibb lettuce
½ pound crabmeat
Pinch of salt and freshly ground pepper
3 tablespoons cognac

Make 2 quarts of *court bouillon* and while the broth is simmering, prepare the crayfish. They must be deveined while still alive. This is done by
holding each crayfish, head first, in one hand and lifting the central tail fin
back toward the head with the other hand. Gently twist the fin left, then
right, and then pull straight back; the intestines will come out. When all
the crayfish are deveined, place them in a colander and rinse with cold
water.

Drop the crayfish in the boiling *court bouillon* and cook for five minutes after the broth begins to boil again. Lift them out with a slotted spoon to cool. Reserve 2 cups of the broth.

Set aside 6 large crayfish. These will be used to decorate the plates. Sever the crayfish tail from the body, and remove the tail meat from the shell. Cover and refrigerate the crayfish meat and the six whole crayfish. Use the crayfish heads, claws, and shells to make the sauce, as follows.

Heat the olive oil in a large heavy saucepan. Add the onions, carrots, leeks, celery, and shallots. Simmer covered, for 10 minutes over medium heat, stirring often. Add the reserved crayfish remains and continue cooking another 5 minutes. Pour in the sherry and white wine and bring to a boil. Add the 2 cups of reserved broth, tomato purée, herbs, pepper, and garlic clove. Cover and boil gently for 30 minutes.

While the sauce is boiling, prepare the *beurre manié* by thoroughly creaming the softened butter and flour together with a fork.

Pour the broth through a fine strainer, into a small saucepan. Use the ladle to force out as much stock as possible. There should be 1¾ cups of liquid. Bring to a boil and stir in the *beurre manié* with a whisk. Gently boil, uncovered for 10 minutes. Remove from the heat. Blend in the 1 teaspoon butter, cream, and cognac. Taste for seasoning and keep warm.

To prepare the molds, preheat oven to 400 degrees.

Generously butter 6 4-ounce ovenproof ramekins. Fit a pastry bag with a large plain tip and fill with the pike mousse. Pipe the mousse into the bottom and onto the sides of the ramekins, forming a "nest" for the crabmeat. The coating should be approximately ½ inch thick all around. Refrigerate the remaining mousse.

Melt 2 tablespoons of butter in a large sauté pan. When the foam subsides, sauté the shallots for about 30 seconds. Then add the shredded lettuce and wilt, approximately one minute. Add the crabmeat, reserved crayfish tails, the pinch of salt, and the pepper, tossing the mixture several times.

Flambé with the 3 tablespoons of cognac.

Moisten the mixture with ⅓ cup of sauce and bring to a boil. Immediately remove from the heat.

Fill the mousseline nests with the crab and crayfish mixture, approximately 2 tablespoons to each. Mound the remaining mousse over the filling, completely encasing it.

Place the filled ramekins in a shallow baking pan. Fill the pan half full with warm water, set on the stove, and bring to a boil over high heat. Transfer the pan to the oven and bake until the mousse just begins to brown, about 12 minutes. Remove from the oven and lift the ramekins out of the water bath.

Unmold by inverting into the center of individual ovenproof plates. Garnish each plate with one of the reserved crayfish, dividing any remaining crabmeat equally. Place the plates in the oven for a few minutes to heat. Coat each mousseline with the warm sauce and serve at once.

Monsieur François's hints to the home cook: You may substitute lobster meat for the crab. Prepare the mousseline using only one type of shellfish.

Croustade de Fruits de Mer à la Pointe de Safran

Seafood in a Saffron Sauce Served in Patty Shells

Serves 4

⅓ pound bay scallops
⅓ pound shrimp, peeled and deveined
4 tablespoons butter
1 tablespoon finely minced shallots
½ pound fresh white mushrooms, cleaned and quartered
1 cup dry white wine
2 tablespoons lemon juice
Large pinch of saffron
Beurre Manié consisting of 2 tablespoons each softened butter and
    all-purpose flour
½ cup heavy whipping cream
½ pound jumbo lump crabmeat
¼ teaspoon salt
Pinch of freshly ground pepper
4 teaspoons sherry
4 large patty shells, 3 inches in diameter
Freshly chopped chives or parsley

Wash the scallops and shrimp in cold water and drain well.

Melt the butter in a large saucepan over medium heat. When the foam subsides add the shallots and sauté for a few moments; do not brown. Add the mushrooms and cook until they are tender, 2 to 3 minutes. Pour in the white wine and lemon juice and bring to a boil. Add the scallops and shrimp. As soon as the liquid comes to a full boil, remove the shrimp, scallops, and mushrooms with a slotted spoon. Cover the seafood with a damp towel to prevent drying and set aside.

Preheat the oven to 300 degrees.

Blend the 2 tablespoons softened butter with the flour thoroughly to make the *beurre manié*. With a whisk, stir it into the boiling liquid, add the saffron, lower the heat, and boil gently for 5 to 8 minutes. Stir occasionally to prevent lumps from forming. Pour any juices that have accumulated in the bowl containing the seafood and mushrooms into the sauce. Add the heavy cream, boil for a minute or two, and remove from heat.

Carefully stir in the crabmeat, scallops, shrimp, and mushrooms. Season with the salt, pepper, and 2 teaspoons sherry. Taste and adjust seasonings.

Place the patty shells on a baking sheet. Pour ½ teaspoon sherry in each and set in the oven for 4 to 5 minutes. Heat four ovenproof plates and place a warmed patty shell on each. Fill patties with the seafood, allowing the sauce to run over the sides of the shell and onto the plate. Sprinkle with the chives or parsley and serve at once.

Monsieur François's finishing touch: Place fresh steamed mussels (page 30) around the filled patty shell just before serving.

Crevettes et St Jacques
à la nage

Shrimp and Scallops in Aromatic Broth

Serves 4

½ cup finely julienned celery
½ cup finely julienned carrots
½ cup finely julienned leeks
½ cup finely shredded onions
1 quart of water
½ cup white wine
2 tablespoons red wine vinegar
1 tablespoon salt
¼ teaspoon freshly ground pepper
1 *bouquet garni* consisting of 2 bay leaves, 4 cloves, ¼ teaspoon cracked
   black peppercorns (see hint on page 4), a pinch of thyme, and
   ⅓ teaspoon coriander seeds, wrapped in cheesecloth
1¼ pounds sea scallops, cut in half if very large
1½ pounds medium shrimp

Combine the vegetables with all the ingredients except the shrimp and scallops in a heavy 3-quart saucepan and place over high heat. Bring the liquid to a boil; lower the heat and simmer for 30 minutes.

Peel and devein the shrimp. Rinse them and the scallops under cold running water.

Before serving, drop the shrimp and scallops into the boiling broth and place over high heat. As soon as the liquid returns to a boil, remove pan from the heat.

Using a slotted spoon, place equal amounts of the shrimp, scallops, and julienne vegetables in four warm bowls. Cover with the hot broth and serve at once.

Monsieur François's hints to the home cook: Prepare the broth anytime that is convenient during the day. Reheat the broth and cook the seafood just before serving. Sprinkle some finely chopped herbs such as parsley, tarragon, or basil on the broth as it leaves the kitchen.

Fricassée de Homard, Crevettes et St-Jacques du Pêcheur

Seafood Fricassee

The ability to taste a sauce, recognize its deficiencies and correct the seasoning, adding a pinch of this or a drop of that to bring out the utmost flavor, makes the cook truly an artist. A recipe can only advise; the necessity of a final decision based on culinary expertise is what raises cooking to the level of an art.

While perfecting his art as a *saucier* in the kitchen of Paris' Plaza Athenée, François befriended Leon, the *chef pâtissier* and a fellow Alsatian. Leon was a gregarious fellow who seemed to enjoy discussing culinary theory. However, it soon became apparent that his questions concerning the amount of cognac necessary to season a portion of lobster bisque properly were not entirely in the pursuit of knowledge! When the two cooks became friends, Leon slyly noted that he preferred his morning coffee laced with a shot of brandy. Conveniently, François enjoyed dunking a freshly baked croissant in his *café au lait*. A mutually satisfying deal was struck.

In order to make this exchange *sans* the detection of the sharp-eyed chef, Leon would arrive with a half-filled coffee cup in hand, and place it directly behind the pot of lobster bisque. François would feign pouring cognac into the sauce, while actually topping off Leon's cup. Leon would then pick up his cup and leave a warm croissant in its place. He returned to the *pâtisserie* with his embellished coffee, leaving Papa to enjoy his *petit déjeuner*.

Serves 4

1 cup *sauce Américaine* (page 38)
2 1-pound live lobsters
8 pearl onions, peeled
8 carrot sticks, ½ inch by 1 inch
8 small broccoli spears
8 asparagus tips
16 green beans
16 snow peas
2 quarts water
2 tablespoons salt
1 pound raw shrimp with shells (16–20 count)
½ pound bay scallops
3 tablespoons butter
1 tablespoon minced shallots
16 small whole white mushrooms
½ cup Sauterne, or a sweet, very fruity white wine
⅓ cup heavy cream
1 teaspoon finely chopped dill
1 tablespoon cognac

Make the *sauce Américaine* with the 2 lobsters. Reserve the lobster meat.

While the sauce is simmering, prepare the vegetables. Bring the water with the 2 tablespoons of salt to a boil. Have a bowl of ice water next to the stove. Cook each vegetable in turn, lift from the boiling water, and plunge into the cold water. The following is a rough guide to approximate cooking time for the vegetables (the time will vary with the size of the vegetables): onions, 8 minutes; carrots, 5 minutes; broccoli, 4 minutes; asparagus, 4 minutes; beans, 3 minutes; and snow peas, 2 minutes.

Let the vegetables cool completely and drain thoroughly.

Peel, devein, and rinse the raw shrimp under cold water. (Reserve the shells in the freezer for shrimp bisque, page 12).

Rinse the scallops under cold water. Drain the shrimp and scallops in a colander.

Preheat the oven to 350 degrees.

Melt the butter in a large saucepan over moderate heat. Add the shallots and simmer for 1 minute. Do not let them brown. Add the mushrooms and sauté for 3 minutes. Add the shrimp and sauté, stirring often, until they begin to redden, approximately 3 to 4 minutes. Add the bay scallops and Sauterne. Bring to a boil over high heat and immediately remove the mushrooms, shrimp, and scallops with a slotted spoon. Keep warm.

Reduce the liquid by two-thirds and add the *sauce Américaine*. Allow the sauce to boil. Remove from the flame and stir in the cream, chopped dill, and cognac. Adjust seasonings.

To serve, arrange ½ lobster, 4 to 5 shrimp, and ¼ of the scallops on each of four ovenproof dinner plates. Divide the prepared vegetables equally. Heat the plates in a warm oven for 3 to 4 minutes. Remove from oven and coat lightly with the sauce. Serve immediately. Serve any extra sauce separately.

Monsieur François's hints to the home cook: To keep the seafood warm while finishing the sauce, see the note on page 71. Substitute your favorite vegetables for those suggested in the recipe.

Melon Farci au Crabe

Melon Stuffed with Crabmeat

Serves 4

1 pound jumbo lump crabmeat
4 tablespoons plus 4 teaspoons mayonnaise (page 52)
½ teaspoon dry mustard
3 tablespoons finely chopped celery
1½ tablespoons finely chopped onion
1 tablespoon finely chopped parsley
¾ tablespoon lemon juice
2 drops Tabasco sauce
6 drops Worcestershire sauce
½ teaspoon salt
¼ teaspoon freshly ground pepper
2 medium cantaloupes
4 slices pimento
16 black olives

Pick through the crabmeat, discarding any pieces of shell but being careful to leave the lumps as intact as possible.

In a small bowl, whisk together 4 tablespoons mayonnaise, mustard, celery, onion, parsley, lemon juice, Tabasco sauce, Worcestershire sauce, salt, and pepper. Add the crabmeat and toss gently. Taste for seasoning.

Cut each melon in half at the "equator" and scrape out all the seeds. Use a melon baller or teaspoon to cut out bite-sized pieces of flesh from the top half of each hemisphere. Mound the pieces back into each melon half.

Mound equal portions of the crabmeat salad on each melon half. Then top with 1 teaspoon of mayonnaise and a pimento slice. Place 4 olives around the crabmeat, just inside the perimeter of the melon.

Monsieur François's hints to the home cook: Prepare the crabmeat ahead of time, but cut and stuff the cantaloupes only a few minutes before serving. Serve with vegetable salads, cucumber (page 139) and beet (page 140), and hardboiled eggs.

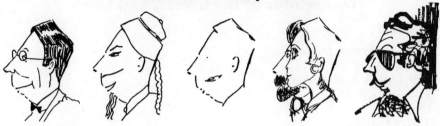

Les Mignons de Bœuf,
Veau et Agneau Gourmandise

Tenderloins of Beef, Veal, and Lamb

Serves 4

1½ pounds veal tenderloin
1½ pounds lamb loin
1½ pounds beef tenderloin
Salt and pepper
Flour
1 stick butter
4 tablespoons vegetable oil
4 teaspoons finely minced shallots
2 teaspoons finely minced garlic
2 teaspoons finely chopped parsley
2 teaspoons lemon juice
1 pound mushrooms, washed and quartered

Sauce:
¼ cup dry white wine
1 teaspoon finely minced shallots
⅛ teaspoon cracked black peppercorns (see hint on page 4)
1 cup basic veal or beef sauce (page 39)
1 tablespoon butter
Pinch of finely minced garlic
2 to 3 drops lemon juice
Salt

Preheat oven to 350 degrees.

Trim any fat and silver skin from all of the tenderloins. Slice each loin into 8 medallions, approximately ½ inch thick. Lightly pound the veal to ¼ inch thickness, as you would for veal scallopini. Season all the medallions with salt and pepper, and dredge only the veal in the flour, shaking off the excess.

Sauté the three meats individually as follows: Using a heavy skillet, melt 1 tablespoon of the butter and 1 tablespoon of the oil over high heat. When the butter begins to brown, quickly sear the veal. Brown one side, then turn and brown the other, approximately 1½ minutes per side. Just before removing the meat, scatter 1 teaspoon shallots, and ½ teaspoon of garlic over the meat; toss several times, allowing the shallots and garlic to cook a few moments. Sprinkle ½ teaspoon each of the parsley and lemon juice on the meat, toss once or twice and transfer the meat to a shallow platter. Wipe out the pan and sauté the lamb and the beef in the same manner.

Lastly, heat 1 tablespoon of butter and 1 tablespoon of oil over a high heat. Sauté the mushrooms 3 to 4 minutes, season with salt and pepper, and add the remaining shallots, garlic, parsley, and lemon juice in the same sequence as for the meats.

To prepare the sauce, pour the fat out of the skillet in which the meats were prepared. Add the shallots, wine, and peppercorns; place over high heat and reduce to a glaze. Add the veal sauce and bring to a boil. Remove from the heat; stir in butter, garlic, and lemon juice with a whisk. Adjust seasonings and keep warm.

Alternate the six slices of meat down the center of each ovenproof plate. Divide the mushrooms evenly around the meats.

Warm the plates in the oven for a minute or two.

Pour 2 to 3 tablespoons of the warm sauce around the meat. Serve the extra sauce separately in a warm sauce boat.

Serve with *carrottes glacés* (page 150) and *pommes sautées Lyonnaise* (page 152).

Monsieur François's hint to the home cook: For a simpler version of this dish use only one kind of meat.

La Longe et Filet d'Agneau
au Fenouil

Loin and Tenderloin of Lamb with Braised Fennel

Serves 6

Saddle of lamb, 5½ to 6 pounds
1½ cups lamb sauce (page 44)
3 medium-sized fennel bulbs
2 tablespoons butter
Salt and pepper
2 tablespoons vegetable oil

Debone the saddle, discarding the fat. Separate the loins and tenderloins, and remove the silver skin. Cover and refrigerate the lamb. Use the bones and trimmings to prepare the lamb stock and lamb sauce.

To prepare the fennel, preheat the oven to 375 degrees. Remove the stalks and any dark outer pieces from the fennel bulbs. Bring a large 2-quart pot of salted water to a boil, drop in the bulbs, and parboil for 10 minutes. Remove from the water and cut each bulb in half. Butter a small baking pan, just large enough to hold the bulb halves in a single layer. Pour ⅔ cup of lamb sauce over the fennel, cover, and bake for 15 to 20 minutes, until tender yet slightly crisp. Remove from the oven and keep warm while cooking the lamb.

To prepare the lamb, salt and pepper the lamb.

Heat the 2 tablespoons of oil in a large skillet over high flame. When the oil begins to smoke, add the pieces of lamb and sear on all sides. Use tongs to turn the lamb rather than piercing the meat with a fork. Lower the flame and cook the tenderloin 4 minutes and the loins 8 minutes for medium rare. Transfer the meat to a warm platter and allow a minimum of 5 minutes before slicing.

Pour the oil out of the pan and add the remaining lamb sauce. Bring to a full boil and keep warm.

Slice the lamb on an angle, not more than ¼ inch thick. Arrange the slices on six warm plates and garnish each with a half fennel bulb.

If the meat is too rare, place the plate under the broiler for a minute or two.

Pour the hot sauce around the meat and serve.

Monsieur François's hints to the home cook: Garnish the lamb with glazed carrots (page 150), sautéed sugar snap peas (page 151) and *tomates provençale* (page 157).

Châteaubriand Banquetière

Châteaubriand with Vegetables

Serves 2

Garnishes:
Glazed Carrots and Onions (page 150)
Sautéed Fresh String Beans (page 149)
Cooked Mushrooms (page 160)
Sautéed Potatoes (page 152)
Baked Tomatoes with Herbs (page 157)
Béarnaise Sauce (page 50)

Meat:
1 18- to 20-ounce center cut of beef tenderloin
1 teaspoon salt
1 teaspoon cracked black peppercorns (see hint on page 4)
1 tablespoon butter
1 tablespoon oil

Prepare the garnishes and Béarnaise sauce.

Trim any fat and silver skin that covers the meat. Place the meat, large end up, in the center of a dish towel. Wrap the towel tightly around the meat. Gather the loose ends of the towel and grasp firmly to securely hold the meat upright.

Pound the "Château" with the flat side of a meat cleaver to approximately half of the original height. The flatter and more cylindrical the shape, the easier it is to cook and slice the meat.

Season the meat with salt and cracked black peppercorns. Heat the butter and oil in a heavy skillet over high heat. When the butter browns, sear the meat well on both sides. Lower the flame slightly and cook the meat a total of 16 minutes for medium rare. Using tongs, turn the meat several times to ensure even cooking.

Preheat oven to 375 degrees.

Remove the meat from the pan and let it rest 5 to 10 minutes before serving. Arrange the vegetables in clusters around the sides of a large ovenproof platter. Carve the meat on a slant into 3/8-inch slices and arrange down the center of the platter. Place the prepared platter in the oven for 2 to 3 minutes to heat all of the vegetables.

Monsieur François's finishing touch: Present the platter at tableside and serve the Châteaubriand on warm plates, accompanied by the Béarnaise sauce.

Monsieur François's hint to the home cook: Cooking meat to the exact degree of doneness takes much practice. Therefore, I suggest you always undercook it slightly. If, after slicing the "Château," you find it underdone, reconstitute the meat, place it on an ovenproof platter, and set in a hot oven for a few minutes.

Escalopes de Veau du Patron

Veal Scallopini

Serves 4

1 ½ pounds veal scallopini cut from the top round, 2 slices per person
Salt and pepper
Flour
½ stick butter
2 teaspoons vegetable oil

Cream and mushroom sauce:
⅓ stick butter
½ pound sliced white mushrooms
½ teaspoon salt
Pinch of freshly ground pepper
¼ cup dry white wine
½ cup basic veal sauce (page 39)
⅓ cup heavy whipping cream
2 tablespoons sherry
Pinch of fresh tarragon leaves

Pound each slice of veal to a thickness of ⅛ to ¼ inch using the flat side of a meat cleaver. Season both sides with salt and pepper. Dredge in the flour, shaking off the excess.

Heat half of the butter with 1 teaspoon of the oil in a large sauté skillet over high heat. When the butter begins to brown, sauté half of the veal until it is lightly browned on both sides. Be certain that the pan is very hot, so that the cooking time is only about 1 minute per side. (Overcooking will toughen the meat.) Sauté the remaining veal. Place the cooked meat on a warm platter and prepare the sauce.

Once the scallopini are cooked, melt the ⅓ stick of butter in the same skillet. Add the mushrooms, salt and pepper. Sauté 3 or 4 minutes, stirring occasionally, until the mushrooms are soft. Pour in the white wine and bring to a boil. Add the brown sauce and heavy cream. Boil several minutes and remove from the heat. Stir in the sherry and tarragon. Taste and adjust seasonings.

Pour the sauce over the warm veal and serve.

Monsieur François's finishing touch: For a tastier sauce, substitute wild mushrooms, such as chanterelles, for half of the white mushrooms. Garnish the veal with julienned and sautéed apples and/or carrots.

Entrecôte au Poivre et Roquefort

Pepper Steak with Roquefort Cheese

All the French waiters say it; all the French chefs say it: "Ordering a *peeper* steak!" Traditionally a cook does not correct *monsieur le chef*. However, I felt it my duty to inform him that, in America, a peeper is a voyeur. I said, "Zee peeper is zee guy hoo looks throux zee weendow at zee peeple hoo ar making zee amour." My lesson did little to change his hard core accent, but I did detect mirth in his voice whenever he ordered the dish.

Who says the French don't care what they say, as long as they pronounce it correctly?

Serves 2

2 New York strip steaks, 12 ounces each
Salt
1 tablespoon cracked black peppercorns (see hint on page 4)
1 tablespoon coarsely ground coriander seeds
2 tablespoons butter
1 tablespoon vegetable oil
2 tablespoons Roquefort cheese

Sauce:
1 teaspoon minced shallots
⅛ teaspoon cracked peppercorns
¼ cup dry white wine
1 cup basic beef sauce (page 39)
1 teaspoon butter
Pinch of minced garlic
2 drops lemon juice
Salt and pepper

Preheat the broiler. Lightly salt the steaks.

Combine the peppercorns and coriander. Using the heel of your hand, firmly press the mixture into both sides of each steak.

Heat the butter and oil in a heavy skillet. When the butter begins to brown, add the steaks and cook over moderately high heat until they are browned on both sides. Allow 3 minutes per side for medium rare.

Remove steaks and place on a platter, keeping them warm while you prepare the sauce.

Wipe out the saucepan in which the steaks were prepared. Then put in the shallots, peppercorns, and wine, and place over high heat. Let the mixture reduce until it is almost dry. Add the beef sauce and bring to a boil. Remove from the heat and stir in the butter with a whisk. Add the garlic and lemon juice. Taste and adjust seasonings.

When ready to serve, place 1 tablespoon of cheese, broken into four or five pieces, on top of each steak.

Place the steaks under the broiler until the cheese begins to melt. Remove the steaks from the broiler and pour the sauce around them. Serve at once.

Choucroute Garnie Alsacienne

Alsatian-Style Sauerkraut with Sausage and Pork

The initiation of neophytes is an honored practice in all professions. Young cooks too must endure certain rites of passage to earn membership in the culinary fellowship.

One morning, early in Papa's apprenticeship, the chef ordered him to take a cord, go down to the cellar, and string up strands of sauerkraut. Papa was familiar with *choucroute*, a traditional Alsatian dish his mother often prepared. He saw her hang socks on the line, but never *choucroute*. However, he dared not ask the chef for an explanation; an apprentice does what he is told unquestioningly. The reasons became apparent later.

After being chided to hurry, Papa filled a pail with sauerkraut and, cord in hand, went down to the cellar. The steep stone steps were slick from seeping water. A single bare light bulb in the high vaulted ceiling barely repelled the darkness. Papa found nails pounded into the ancient cellar walls, no doubt from previous sauerkraut hangings. He secured several strands of cord across the room and began his assignment. After a frustrating hour of labor, he climbed back to the kitchen only to be greeted by patronizing guffaws from the entire staff, a kick in the *derrière*, and a severe reprimand from the chef.

Serves 6

5 pounds sauerkraut
3 tablespoons rendered goose fat or lard (see hint on page 119)
2 medium-sized onions, diced
1 large apple, peeled and finely diced
½ teaspoon salt
1½ cups dry white wine (preferably Alsatian Riesling)
1 cup chicken stock (page 115)
1 *bouquet garni* consisting of 3 cloves, 1 bay leaf, 3 garlic cloves crushed,
    ½ teaspoon thyme, 12 crushed juniper berries, and 10 cracked black
    peppercorns (see hint on page 4), wrapped in cheesecloth
1- to 2-pound slab smoked bacon
2 pounds smoked pork shoulder
12 small potatoes
Salt
1 teaspoon oil
6 bratwurst
6 frankfurters
2 pounds polish kielbasa
Horseradish
Dijon mustard

Preheat oven to 350 degrees.
    Place the sauerkraut in a large colander and rinse with cold water. Wring with your hands to remove as much moisture as possible.
    Melt the lard in a deep, heavy saucepan and cook the onions and apple until limp, but do not brown. Add the sauerkraut, salt, wine, and chicken

stock. Bring to a full boil. Bury the *bouquet garni* in the sauerkraut along with the slab of bacon and pork shoulder. Cover and cook in the preheated oven for 1 ½ hours. The sauerkraut should still be slightly firm.

While the sauerkraut is cooking, boil the potatoes in a pot of salted water for 20 to 30 minutes, or until tender. Peel and keep warm.

Heat the oil in a small pan and brown the bratwurst over low heat. Set aside and keep warm.

Heat the frankfurters and kielbasa by burying them in the hot sauerkraut for 10 to 15 minutes before removing the pan from the oven. Taste sauerkraut for seasoning, add salt if necessary.

Remove the pork and bacon from the saucepan and cut into thick slices. Place the sauerkraut on a large oval or rectangular platter. Arrange the pork and bacon slices with the sausages and boiled potatoes on top. Serve with the horseradish and Dijon mustard.

Monsieur François's finishing touch: For a more festive sauerkraut, serve with slices of roast goose (page 118), sections of roast duck (page 116), or roast pheasant (page 121). Heat the poultry with the sausages a few minutes before serving.

Monsieur François's hint for the home cook: Prepare the sauerkraut ahead and reheat it before serving. Pour a few tablespoons of white wine in a heavy saucepan. Add the sauerkraut and sausages, cover, and place over low heat until hot, 5 to 8 minutes.

Asperges Fraiches à notre façon

Alsatian-Style Fresh Asparagus

Serves 4

2 quarts water
2 tablespoons salt
2 pounds fresh jumbo asparagus
4 veal scallopini, cut from the top round
Salt and freshly ground black pepper
All-purpose flour
1 stick butter
1 tablespoon vegetable oil
4 slices dry cured ham
1 tablespoon red wine vinegar
2 teaspoons capers
8 tablespoons grated Gruyère cheese
2 hard-boiled eggs
4 sprigs fresh parsley

In a saucepan combine the water with the salt, bay leaves, and cloves and simmer for 15 minutes.

Meanwhile, peel the asparagus and cut off the tough lower stems. Lay the asparagus in a deep pan so that all the tips are facing in the same direction. Cover the asparagus with the seasoned water, bring to a boil and simmer 5 to 6 minutes. Drain at once on towels.

Preheat the broiler.

Pound the veal to an even thickness of ¼ inch with the flat side of a meat cleaver. Season with salt and pepper and dredge in flour, shaking off the excess. In a large sauté pan, combine 2 tablespoons of the butter and 1 tablespoon oil over high flame until the butter begins to brown. Add the veal and sauté quickly on both sides until lightly browned, 1 to 2 minutes. Remove the veal and keep warm. Add the slices of ham and lightly sauté, about 20 seconds on each side.

Place a slice of veal and a slice of ham side by side on warm dinner plates. Arrange the asparagus on top of the meats and sprinkle with the vinegar and capers. Top with the grated cheese. Place the prepared plates under the broiler to brown the cheese.

Brown the remaining butter. Remove the plates from the broiler and pour the browned butter over the asparagus. Garnish each plate with two quarters of hard-boiled egg and a sprig of fresh parsley. Serve at once.

Monsieur François's hint to the home cook: Use your favorite grated cheese in place of the Gruyère. Note, some are rather salty and must be used accordingly.

Jarret de Veau Braisé

Braised Veal Shanks

Serves 4

8 meaty veal shanks (1–1 ½ inches thick)
1 tablespoon salt
1 teaspoon freshly ground pepper
⅓ cup flour
½ cup vegetable oil
¾ cup finely chopped onions
½ cup finely diced carrots
1 cup dry white wine
½ pound mushrooms, cleaned and quartered
2 cups *fonds brun* (page 39)
⅓ cup tomato purée
1 bay leaf
2 cloves
¼ teaspoon thyme
2 garlic cloves, peeled and crushed
¼ teaspoon garlic, minced
1 tablespoon sherry

Preheat oven to 375 degrees.

Salt and pepper the veal shanks and dredge in flour, shaking off the excess. In a small heavy roasting pan or Dutch oven, heat ¼ cup of the vegetable oil over high heat. Add the shanks and brown well on both sides, 4 to 5 minutes per side. Remove from the pan and set aside. (It may be necessary to brown the shanks in two batches.)

Add the remaining oil to the pan and sauté the onions and carrots over moderate heat until lightly browned. Return the shanks to the pan, add the white wine, and bring to a boil. Then add the mushrooms, brown sauce, tomato purée, herbs, and 2 garlic cloves. Bring to a boil, cover, and place in the oven. Turn down heat and simmer for 2 to 3 hours, stirring occasionally, until meat can easily be pierced with a fork.

Remove from oven, stir in the minced garlic and sherry and adjust seasonings.

Arrange shanks on a heated plate. Coat with sauce and garnish with glazed carrots and onions (page 150).

Monsieur François's hint to the home cook: Don't forget to scoop the marrow out of the bone; spread it on a piece of bread and enjoy.

Ris de Veau Braisés Françillon

Braised Sweetbreads

In the early days of Chez François few people appreciated sweetbreads and they were sold at market for almost nothing. Quite a contrast from the expensive delicacy of today.

Serves 6

3 pounds veal sweetbreads
Salt and pepper
Flour
4 tablespoons butter
2 tablespoons oil
½ cup finely chopped onions
1 tablespoon finely chopped shallots
1 cup dry white wine
½ teaspoon finely chopped garlic
1 bay leaf
2 cloves
2 tablespoons tomato purée
½ pound quartered mushrooms
2 cups *fonds brun* (page 39)
¼ cup sherry

Degorge the sweetbreads by placing them in a bowl of cold water and refrigerate overnight. Change the water several times.

Drain the sweetbreads, place in a large pot, and cover with water. Bring to a boil over high heat and blanch for 5 minutes. Transfer the pot to the sink and cool the sweetbreads under cold running water.

Drain the sweetbreads, peel off the outer membrane, and cut away any veins and dark spots. Slice each lobe into 2 to 3 pieces, 1 inch thick.

Pat the sweetbreads dry with paper towels. Sprinkle the slices with salt and pepper and dust with flour, shaking off excess. Heat 2 tablespoons of the butter and 1 tablespoon of the oil in a large skillet; when the butter begins to brown, add the sweetbreads and brown lightly on all sides. This will require two batches. When the second batch is done, add the onions and shallots and sauté with the sweetbreads for a few seconds. Transfer to a flameproof casserole.

Place the casserole over moderate heat. Add the wine and boil for 1 minute. Add the chopped garlic, bay leaf, cloves, tomato purée, mushrooms, and brown sauce (just enough to cover the sweetbreads). Cover the pot, allowing it to simmer for 20 minutes. The sweetbreads are done when a sharp knife passes easily through the meat.

Remove from the stove and add the sherry. Taste and adjust seasonings.

Monsieur François's finishing touch: For a smoother sauce, add a teaspoon or two of butter and mix well. Serve the sweetbreads with glazed carrots (page 150) and sautéed sugar snap peas (page 151).

Ris de Veau aux Champignons Sauvages

Sautéed Sweetbreads with Chanterelle Mushrooms

Serves 4

2 to 2½ pounds veal sweetbreads
Salt and pepper
All-purpose flour
4 tablespoons butter
4 tablespoons oil

Mushrooms:
1 pound fresh or 3 ounces dry chanterelle mushrooms
2 tablespoons olive oil
¾ teaspoon finely minced shallots
1 tablespoon freshly chopped parsley
Sauce Charcutière (page 41)

Begin the day before you intend to serve this dish by covering the sweet-breads in cold water to degorge. Refrigerate overnight, changing the water once or twice.

If using dried mushrooms, soak them in cold water for 24 hours, changing the water two or three times.

The following day, drain the sweetbreads, place in a large saucepan and cover with cold water. Bring to a boil, reduce the heat, and blanch for 5 to 8 minutes. Transfer the pan to the sink, cool the sweetbreads under cold running water, and drain well in a colander.

Remove the fat, gristle, and outer membrane from the sweetbreads. Slice into scallops approximately ⅓ to ½ inch thick.

Preheat oven to 400 degrees.

Season the sweetbread slices with salt and pepper, dust lightly with flour, and shake off the excess. Heat the butter and oil in a large heavy skillet; when the butter browns, sauté the sweetbreads 1 to 2 minutes per side until golden brown. Transfer the skillet to the oven and bake 3 to 4 minutes.

Sauté the chanterelles in the olive oil and add the shallots and parsley according to the directions for sautéed wild mushrooms (page 151). Heat the *sauce charcutière*, set aside and keep warm.

Remove the sweetbreads from the oven. Divide them evenly and arrange in a circle design on four warm dinner plates. Scatter the mushrooms over the sweetbreads and set the plates in the oven for a minute or two to heat. Pour the sauce around the meat and serve at once.

Monsieur François's finishing touch: Use any of the many varieties of wild mushrooms either singularly or mixed (see hint page 27).

Côtes de Veau Farcies Strasbourgeoise

Alsatian-Style Stuffed Veal Chops

Serves 4

Stuffing:
6 ounces boneless veal
2 ounces duck *foie gras* (See hint on page 16)
¾ teaspoon salt
¼ teaspoon freshly ground pepper
⅛ teaspoon ground nutmeg
1 teaspoon brandy
2 tablespoons heavy whipping cream
2 teaspoons freshly chopped parsley
1 teaspoon chopped truffles (optional)

Veal:
4 1-inch thick veal chops
salt and freshly ground pepper
flour
1 tablespoon vegetable oil
1 tablespoon butter
2 tablespoons freshly chopped onion
1 cup basic veal sauce (page 39)
1 tablespoon Madeira

To prepare the stuffing, cube the veal and place in a food processor with the *foie gras*, salt, pepper, nutmeg, and brandy. Process for about 1 minute to form a course paste. Add the cream, parsley, and truffles and process for ten more seconds. Taste and adjust the seasoning and refrigerate.

When purchasing the veal chops for the recipe, select "prime" or "first" chops, i.e. those located near the saddle end of the rack of veal, as they are the meatiest with the largest "eyes." The chops will probably require some trimming at home.

With a meat cleaver, cut the rib bone to a length of no more than three inches above the "eye." Cut and scrape the meat and fat from the top three inches of the rib. Remove all but a thin layer of fat around the "eyes" and leave all but a small chunk of fat above the "eyes" along the rib. Lightly pound the veal chops with the side of a meat cleaver. Use the bones and trimmings in the preparation of the veal sauce.

To prepare the veal, place a veal chop flat on the work surface in front of you, the rib bone should be pointing towards you with the "eye" to the right side of the bone. Place the palm of your left hand over the length of the rib bone to hold the chop in position. Using a thin sharp boning knife, form a "pocket" in the chop by making a small incision (approximately ¾ inch wide) in the top of the "eye," one inch to the right of the rib. Hold the knife parallel to the work surface and insert the blade (cutting-edge facing the bone) three-quarters of the way down the right side of the "eye." Keep the blade about ½ inch away from the side and bottom of the chop. Be careful not to pierce through the sides. Keeping the knife level, pivot the blade towards the rib (right to left), stopping the slice ½ inch before the rib.

Place the stuffing in a pastry bag, fitted with a small plain tube. Insert the top of the tube into the "pocket" and force in the stuffing. Evenly divide the stuffing among the four chops.

Preheat the oven to 425 degrees.

Salt, pepper, and lightly flour the chops. Combine the oil and butter in a large skillet (about 11 inches). Place over high heat, when the butter begins to brown, add the chops and sear on each side for 2 minutes. Transfer the skillet to the oven and cook the veal for 20 minutes. Turn twice while cooking. After 17 minutes, scatter the chopped onion around the chops.

When the veal chops are done, transfer them to a large serving platter and keep warm. Pour the grease out of the skillet, retaining the chopped onion.

Place the skillet over high heat and immediately deglaze with the 1 cup of veal stock. Stir well and scrape the bottom of the skillet to loosen the caramelized juices. Boil the sauce for 2–3 minutes. Remove from the heat and stir in the Madeira.

Taste and adjust seasoning and strain into a sauce boat.

Serve with glazed carrots and onions (see page 150).

Tripes à la Mode de Chez nous

Baked Tripe

A dish not appreciated by all. One to share with close culinary cohorts on a blustery winter day.

Serves 6 to 8

3 pounds honeycomb tripe
3 pig's feet, split in half lengthwise
1 calf's foot, split in half lengthwise
1 cup coarsely diced carrots
4 cups sliced onions
2 cups whole leeks, sliced
¼ cup sliced celery
2 tablespoons tomato purée
1 *bouquet garni* consisting of ¼ teaspoon cracked pepper, 2 bay leaves, 3 cloves, and 2 crushed garlic cloves, wrapped in cheesecloth
1 tablespoon salt
1 quart dry white wine
1 tablespoon sherry
1 tablespoon cognac

Wash the tripe, pig's feet, and calf's foot thoroughly under cold running water. Place in a large stockpot, cover with cold water, bring to a boil, and blanch for 10 minutes. Drain and rinse in cold water.

Preheat oven to 325 degrees.

Cut the tripe into 2-inch pieces and place in a large flameproof casserole or Dutch oven with a tightly fitted lid. Add the pig's feet, calf's foot, vegetables, *bouquet garni*, salt, wine, and enough cold water to just cover all the ingredients. Place over high heat and bring the liquid to a full boil. Cover tightly, set in the oven, and barely simmer for 6 to 7 hours. Check from time to time, adding water as necessary to maintain level. Test for doneness by removing a piece of tripe, cutting, and tasting. It should be very tender. When the tripe is done, pour into a colander set over a bowl.

When cool enough to handle, pick the pieces of tripe out and place them back in the Dutch oven. Remove the pig's feet and calf's foot and separate the meat from the bones, cutting any large pieces. Use your fingers to remove all the small bones from the meat. Return all the meat and liquid in the bowl to the Dutch oven. Bring to a boil on the stove and remove from heat. Add the cognac and sherry; taste and adjust seasonings.

Monsieur François's hint to the home cook: The tripe may be prepared ahead of time and stored in the refrigerator until ready to use. Serve in large soup bowls with boiled potatoes.

Rognons de Veau Moutarde

Veal Kidneys with Mustard Sauce

Let's admit it, the French have a knack for making simply marvelous meals from lowly organ meats.

Serves 4

2 veal kidneys, approximately 12 ounces each
½ pound white mushrooms, cleaned and quartered
Salt and pepper
All-purpose flour
4 tablespoons butter
1 tablespoon oil
1 tablespoon finely minced shallots
4 tablespoons dry white wine
¼ cup basic veal sauce (page 39)
1 cup heavy cream
2 heaping tablespoons Dijon mustard

Remove the outer membrane and as much fat as possible from the kidneys. Split each lengthwise and cut into pieces the size of mushroom quarters.

Melt 2 tablespoons of the butter in a large sauté pan; when the foam subsides, add the mushrooms and cook for 2 to 3 minutes. Season with salt and pepper. Remove from heat, set aside, and wipe the pan clean.

Lightly salt and pepper the kidneys and dust with the flour. Remove the excess flour by placing the kidneys in a small wire strainer and shaking them back and forth. Heat the 2 remaining tablespoons of butter and 1 tablespoon of oil in the same pan used to cook the mushrooms. When the butter begins to brown, sauté the kidneys over high heat for 3 to 4 minutes, shaking the pan frequently so the pieces brown on all sides. Lift the pieces of kidney out of the pan with a slotted spoon and reserve with the mushrooms.

Place the pan over high heat, add the shallots, and cook for 30 seconds. Deglaze with the white wine, scraping the bottom of the pan to dissolve the meat particles. Add the veal sauce, cream, and mustard. Bring to a boil. Taste and adjust seasonings.

Return the mushroom and kidneys to the sauce, heat a few moments, and serve with noodles.

Rognons de Veau au Vinaigre de Xérès

Veal Kidneys with Sherry Wine Vinegar Sauce

Serves 4

½ pound white mushrooms
2 veal kidneys, approximately 12 ounces each
Salt and pepper
All-purpose flour
5 tablespoons butter
1 tablespoon oil
1 tablespoon finely minced shallots
4 tablespoons sherry wine vinegar
½ cup basic veal sauce (page 39)

Wash the mushrooms in several changes of cold water. Lift them out of the water leaving the grit behind. Quarter the mushrooms.

Remove the outer membrane and the fat from the kidneys. Cut the kidneys into pieces approximately the same size as the quartered mushrooms.

Melt 2 tablespoons of the butter in a large sauté pan; when the foam subsides, sauté the mushrooms for 2 to 3 minutes and season with salt and pepper. Set aside and wipe the pan clean.

Lightly season the kidneys with salt and pepper and dust with flour, shaking off the excess. Brown 2 tablespoons of butter with 1 tablespoon of oil over high heat in the same pan used to cook the mushrooms. Sauté the kidneys for 3 to 4 minutes, shaking frequently so the pieces brown on all sides. Lift the pieces of kidney out of the pan with a slotted spoon and reserve with the mushrooms.

Return the pan to the stove and sauté the shallots for 30 seconds. Pour in the sherry wine vinegar, scraping the bottom of the pan to dissolve the meat particles and reduce by half. Add the veal sauce and bring to a boil. Lower the heat and stir in the remaining tablespoon of butter with a whisk. Adjust seasonings.

Heat the mushrooms and kidneys in the sauce. Serve with noodles or spätzle (page 163).

Monsieur François's hints to the home cook: Overcooked kidney is very tough and chewy. Use red wine vinegar if sherry wine vinegar is unavailable.

Cervelle de Veau au Beurre Noir

Calves' Brains with Black Butter

Serves 4

4 sets calves' brains
1 quart *court bouillon* (page 36)
4 teaspoons capers
½ stick butter
1 tablespoon wine vinegar
Lemon wedges

Begin the day before by carefully removing the outer membrane from each set of brains. Place them in a deep bowl and cover with cold water to degorge. Refrigerate overnight.

One hour before serving, prepare the *court bouillon* in a wide pan and have it simmering on top of the stove. Ten minutes before serving, carefully slide the brains into the hot broth. Bring to a boil, simmer for 5 minutes, and remove from the heat.

With the large slotted spoon, carefully lift the brains from the broth and place on warm dinner plates. Scatter the capers over each set of brains.

Melt the butter in a skillet until it turns very dark brown, almost black. Pour the sizzling butter over the brains. Add the vinegar to the hot pan, swirl around once or twice, and pour over the brains. Serve at once, garnished with lemon wedges, boiled potatoes and chopped parsley.

Monsieur François's hint to the home cook: Always buy fresh calves' brains because it is very difficult to peel off the outer membrane from brains that have been previously frozen.

Cervelle de Veau Sautée

Sautéed Calves' Brains

Gosh, with these fancy French names, how's a fellow supposed to know what he's ordering? Can't they just come out and say what all this stuff is? Well, now they have.

In the old days, if Escoffier had written the menu for a Saturday afternoon meal at the ballpark, that all-American favorite would have been called *le saucisson Babe Ruth*.

Today, however, the *Nouvelle Cuisine* chefs have scrapped all "elite" classic menu titles in favor of a more democratic, straight-forward description of each item. A ball park hot dog with relish and catsup might be dubbed *la saucisse de boeuf et porc nitrite pochée a l'eau de la source dans sa robe croustillante au coulis de tomate et confiture de cornichons.*

Now if that's plain talk, I'll eat my chef's hat!

Serves 4

4 sets calves' brains
1 quart *court bouillon* (page 36)
Salt and pepper
All-purpose flour
2 tablespoons plus 1 stick butter
2 tablespoons oil
4 tablespoons capers
1 tablespoon wine vinegar
Lemon wedges

Follow the procedure for poaching the brains in *cervelle de veau au beurre noir* (page 109). Let the brains cool completely in the *court bouillon*. Lift the brains carefully from the broth and pat dry with paper towels.

Preheat oven to 400 degrees. Season the brains with salt and pepper and dredge in flour, shaking off the excess.

Heat the butter and oil in a large sauté pan until the butter begins to brown. Add the brains and sauté until lightly browned, approximately 2 minutes. Turn with a spatula and set the pan in the oven for 5 minutes.

Remove to warm plates and top with the capers. Wipe out the pan and melt the stick of butter until very brown and pour over the brains. Add the vinegar to the hot pan, swirl once or twice, and pour over the sautéed brains. Serve with the lemon wedges and boiled potatoes.

Langue de Boeuf Fumée au Madère

Beef Tongue in Madeira Sauce

Serves 4

1 smoked beef tongue
1 gallon unsalted *court bouillon* (page 36)
2 cups Madeira sauce (page 40)
Wilted spinach (page 152)

The day before cooking the tongue, place it in a deep bowl and cover with cold water. Let the tongue soak overnight in the refrigerator, changing the water twice to remove excess salt.

Prepare the *court bouillon* in a stockpot large enough to accommodate the broth and the beef tongue. Place the tongue in the warm broth and boil gently until the thickest part is easily pierced with a meat fork, about 2½ hours.

Remove the pot from the heat and allow the tongue to cool while submerged in the broth. When cool enough to handle, peel and skin and trim the cartilage and fat from the base of the tongue. Store the tongue in the broth until time to serve.

Heat the Madeira sauce.

Boil 2 cups of the broth in a small saucepan and reduce the heat. Cut thin diagonal slices, place the slices in the broth, and simmer for 1 to 2 minutes. Lift the tongue slices out of the broth and arrange on warm dinner plates. Garnish with wilted spinach and cover the tongue with the hot Madeira sauce. Serve at once.

Monsieur François's finishing touch: Sprinkle chopped gherkins, *cornichons*, on the tongue just before serving.

Les Volailles et Gibiers

Poultry and Game

Coq au Riesling d'Alsace

Chicken in Alsatian Riesling Wine

Among the many dishes in his repertoire, each chef has personal favorites. They may be original creations, or customers' popular requests, or they may involve an expert culinary technique. At Rôtisserie Perigourdine, Chef Jean's favorite, *Coq au Riesling,* required a special technique.

Every Wednesday morning, chef Jean summoned Pierre, the *sommelier,* and reminded him that the *plat du jour* required Riesling. Pierre, in black tie, knowingly acknowledged the chef's request. He bowed, turned and descended into *la cave,* returning a few minutes later with two bottle of vintage Riesling on a silver tray. Pierre presented the bottles to the chef for approval as he would to a guest in the dining room. After a moment's assessment of the bouquet this vintage would impart to the sauce, the chef nodded, indicating his acceptance of the bottles and dismissing Pierre from his presence.

One bottle was used directly in the preparation of the sauce. The other was spirited away to the walk-in refrigerator where it would be properly chilled for the kitchen staff to savor as their pre-dinner *apéritif.* We all relished our roles in this performance. After all, tradition must be maintained.

Serves 4

2 2½-pound chickens
Salt and pepper
All-purpose flour
2 tablespoons butter
1 teaspoon oil
2 tablespoons finely chopped onion
½ cup marinade
½ cup Alsatian Riesling wine
1 cup chicken stock (*fonds de volaille*) (page 115)
3 cups fresh mushrooms, cleaned and quartered
2 tablespoons butter
⅓ cup heavy cream

Marinade:

1½ cups Alsatian Reisling wine
½ cup finely sliced onions
¼ cup finely sliced carrots
1 *bouquet garni* consisting of ¼ teaspoon cracked black
    peppercorns (see hint on page 4), 1 clove of garlic peeled
    and crushed, 2 bay leaves, 4 cloves, and a pinch of thyme,
    wrapped in cheesecloth

Chicken stock:
Reserved carcasses, plus wing parts, necks, and giblets
2 tablespoons oil
Reserved diced onions and carrots
2 tablespoons flour
2½ cups cold water
Reserved *bouquet garni*
½ teaspoon salt

Cut the chickens into quarters, removing the wings at the second joint. Reserve the necks, giblets, carcasses, and wing tips.

Combine the marinade ingredients in a bowl. Add the chicken quarters. Cover and refrigerate overnight.

The following day, lift the chicken parts out of the marinade, thoroughly dry them, and return to the refrigerator. Strain the marinade to separate the liquid, vegetables and *bouquet garni*, reserving all.

To prepare the chicken stock, cut the chicken carcasses into 3 or 4 pieces with a cleaver. In a heavy 6-quart saucepan or Dutch oven, heat the oil over medium flame. Add all the bones and sauté for 10 minutes, stirring occasionally. Do not brown. Add the reserved carrots and onions, and cook an additional 5 minutes.

Dust the bones with the flour and stir thoroughly, scraping the bottom of the pan. Cover the bones with water and bring to a boil. Skim the fat and add the reserved *bouquet garni* and salt. Lower the heat and simmer, uncovered, for 45 minutes to reduce and concentrate the stock. Strain and skim. Approximately 1 cup should remain.

To prepare the chicken, season the marinated parts with salt and pepper and dredge in the flour, shaking off the excess.

Heat the butter and oil in the same pot used to prepare the stock. When the butter browns, sauté the chicken for 3 minutes per side, or until golden brown. As soon as the chicken has browned, remove to a platter. When all the chicken has been sautéed, pour out the grease, add the chopped onions, and return the chicken to the pan.

Boil the reserved marinade in a small pan, skim well, and add to the chicken along with the Riesling wine. Bring to a boil and add the cup of *fonds de volaille*. Cover the pan and simmer for 15 minutes, occasionally shaking the pot.

While the chicken is cooking, sauté the mushrooms in 2 tablespoons of butter, season with salt and pepper, and add to the chicken.

After simmering for 15 minutes, stir in the heavy cream. Taste and adjust seasonings. Serve with noodles or spätzle (page 163).

Monsieur François's hint to the home cook: Prepare the *Coq au Riesling* ahead of time, omitting the cream until just before serving.

Caneton du Long Island Bigarade

Roast Duck with Orange Sauce

"Fire! Fire!" The incidence of arson is on the rise. Though law inforcement officials cite causes ranging from insurance fraud to revenge, the fact remains that the majority of arsonists never are caught nor their motives known, but the *Nouvelle Cuisine* chefs know. . . .

Remember the good old days, when men were men and tuxedoed waiters flambéed every dish at your table? In order to be as spectacular as possible, the waiter used a quarter bottle of liqueur, sending flames several feet in the air. What a show, complete with the oohs and aahs of the dazzled guests. Alas, that is all passé.

At the downtown Chez François, we flambéed several dishes, including the *Caneton Bigarade*, but at L'Auberge we have taken the modern course and stopped flambéing in the dining room. After all, no chef wants his creations tampered with by a waiter.

However, look at the result, *Nouvelle* Arson! The disenflambéed gourmands are sure to discover the source of their frustrations and direct the fire at their tormentors. Chefs, reissue the flambé pans before it is too late!

Serves 4

2 4½- to 5-pound ducks
Salt and pepper
¼ cup vegetable oil
16 orange sections
1 tablespoon sugar
1 cup orange sauce (page 47)

Preheat oven to 450 degrees.

Remove the pouch containing the neck, liver, and giblets and any fat from the duck's cavity. Prick the ducks all over with a fork to allow excess fat to escape. Salt and pepper both inside and outside of the ducks before roasting.

Put the roasting pan in the preheated oven for 5 minutes. Pour the vegetable oil into the pan. Close the oven and allow the oil to heat for 2 minutes.

Place the ducks in the pan, breast side down, and roast for 35 minutes. Reduce the heat to 375 degrees. Pour excess fat out of the pan and reserve. Turn the ducks over, and continue cooking another 30 minutes. The ducks should be nicely browned. Test for doneness by pricking deep into the breast. If the juice runs clear, the bird is ready. Remove the ducks from the pan. Cool slightly and carve into quarters. (Allow half a duck per person.)

Place the orange sections in a low ovenproof dish, sprinkle with sugar, and glaze under the broiler for 3 to 4 minutes.

Arrange duck portions and orange sections on four plates. Heat the plates in the oven for 2 to 3 minutes. Pour 2 to 3 tablespoons of warm orange sauce on each plate and serve.

Aiguillettes de Canard
aux Pommes et Quetsches

Duck Breasts with Apples and Plums

Serves 4

2 4½- to 5-pound ducks
1 cup apple duck sauce (page 48)
1 large apple
8 plums, split in half
6 tablespoon butter
1 tablespoon sugar
1 tablespoon oil
Salt and freshly ground pepper

Completely debone the ducks. Use the bones, sinews, and skin to make the sauce. Leave the breasts whole, removing all but a thin layer of fat and set aside. Reserve the remaining duck meat and half of the fat for the stuffed quail recipe (page 125).

Peel, core, and cut the apple into eight wedges. Split the plums in half lengthwise and remove the pits. Prepare the fruit by melting 2 tablespoons of butter in a small skillet. Add the apple wedges, sprinkle with the sugar, and sauté, tossing frequently, for 4 to 5 minutes until the sugar is lightly caramelized. Sauté the plums in the same manner with 2 tablespoons butter, but do not sweeten unless they are very tart.

Divide the fruit between four ovenproof plates and place in a 200-degree oven. Heat the sauce and then keep warm.

Lightly salt and pepper the duck breasts. In a large skillet, heat the remaining 2 tablespoons of butter and 1 tablespoon of oil. When the butter begins to brown, add the breasts, skin side down. Sauté for 3 minutes. Then turn the breasts and cook an additional 3 minutes for medium rare. Increase the cooking time to suit individual taste. Remove from the pan and allow to rest for 5 minutes. Cut thin diagonal slices and place one on each plate. Pour the sauce around the breast slices and serve.

Monsieur François's hints to the home cook: Debone a duck by placing it breast up with the cavity facing you. Grasp the left thigh, pull it away from the carcass, and then cut down through the joint to separate it. Turn the duck so the neck faces you and remove the other thigh. Remove the breast by running the knife along one side of the breastbone and scraping the meat off along the rib cage. Cut through and detach the wing joint at the shoulder. Repeat on the other side. Finally, cut away the wing joint attached to each breast, leaving two duck "steaks."

Scrape away all the meat from the thigh and leg bones (no need to be neat about it since the flesh will be ground for stuffing) and reserve for the stuffed quail (page 125).

L'Oie Rôtie Farcie aux Marrons

Roast Goose with Chestnut Stuffing

Our recipes require many steps, but do not be deterred. The end results will more than make up for the pile of pots and pans in the sink.

In Papa's youth, apprentices were obliged to polish all the copper pots and pans. The chef, to steel the youngsters to the rigors of their profession, insisted that the kitchenware be spotless. One day while the young cooks were leaving for their usual afternoon break, the chef sprinkled water on the newly shined pots. He called his apprentices back, admonished their shabby work and made them repolish all the pans, foregoing their rest period.

Remember Papa's chef the next time every piece of cookware in the house is dirty. It will lighten your task.

Serves 8
1 goose (8 to 10 pounds)
Salt and pepper
4 tablespoons vegetable oil

Sauce:
2 tablespoons vegetable oil
Goose wings and giblets
1 cup sliced onions
½ cup sliced carrots
1 small piece of celery
1 bay leaf
Pinch of thyme
2 cloves
1 garlic clove, crushed
2 tablespoons flour
1 quart white stock (page 42) or chicken stock (page 115)
1 tablespoon Madeira
¼ teaspoon cracked black peppercorns (see hint on page 4)
1 tablespoon salt
Chestnut stuffing (page 120)

Preheat oven to 450 degrees.

Cut off the wing tips at the second joint. Remove the neck and giblets from the cavity of the goose. Reserve the liver for the *terrine de foie* (see page 24).

Salt the goose inside and out.

Place a roasting pan, just large enough to accommodate the goose, in the oven for 5 minutes. Pour the vegetable oil into the hot roasting pan and carefully place the goose in it, breast side down. Brown for 25 minutes; then turn the goose and lower the heat to 350 degress. Cooking time is between 2 and 2½ hours.

Baste the goose every 30 minutes. Test for doneness by pricking the breast with a fork. The juices should run clear. Begin the sauce as soon as the goose goes into the oven.

To prepare the sauce, heat the vegetable oil in a 3-quart saucepan, add the wing tips, giblets, vegetables, and brown over high heat, stirring often for 10 minutes. Dust with the flour and mix thoroughly. Stir in the stock, bring to a boil, add herbs and garlic, reduce the heat, cover, and simmer while the goose roasts.

When the goose is done, remove it from the oven and set aside. Pour the rendered goose fat out of the roasting pan and reserve. (Goose fat is excellent for sautéing and roasting. It will keep a month or more in the refrigerator.)

Strain the sauce into the roasting pan. Discard all the solids except the giblets. Place the pan on the stove and bring the sauce to a boil. Transfer back into the saucepan and boil again. Skim the fat and reduce the heat.

Dice the giblets and add to the sauce. Add the Madeira and adjust seasonings. Keep warm.

To serve, carve the goose. Place 2 tablespoons of warm chestnut stuffing on each plate. Cover with slices of goose and set in the oven for several minute to warm. Pour the sauce over the slices. Garnish with cranberry sauce (page 56) and braised red cabbage (page 154)

Monsieur François's hint to the home cook: Strain the rendered goose or duck fat and allow to cool. Pour into a container and store in the refrigerator. Duck or goose fat is excellent for sautéing meats and potatoes.

La Farce aux Marrons

Chestnut Stuffing

Serves 10 to 12

1 pound fresh chestnuts
4 tablespoons vegetable oil
½ pound pork shoulder, cubed
½ pound veal, cubed
½ pound pork belly, cubed
1 cup chopped onion
1 cup dried bread
½ cup milk
3 eggs, beaten
2 teaspoons salt
¼ teaspoon freshly ground pepper
⅔ teaspoon pâté spices (page 20)
½ teaspoon minced garlic

Shell and cook the chestnuts, as in the chestnut purée recipe, page 147. There should be approximately 3 cups. (This may be done the previous day.)

Preheat oven to 400 degrees.

Heat 2 tablespoons of the oil in a large skillet over high heat and sauté half of the cubed meat. When the meat is lightly browned, add half of the onions, and continue cooking several minutes. Transfer the meat and onions to a baking pan and cool. Repeat with the remaining meat and onions.

Soak the bread in the milk, adding more milk if necessary to completely moisten. Wring out the bread with your hands, discarding the milk.

Using a fine disc, grind the cooled meat, onions, and bread into a mixing bowl. Add all the ingredients except the chestnuts. Sauté a small patty of stuffing and taste for seasoning, adjusting if necessary.

Mix in the thoroughly drained chestnuts. Place the stuffing in a buttered ovenproof casserole or a loaf pan and cover with foil.

Set the casserole into a small roasting plan two-thirds filled with water. Bring to a boil and transfer to the preheated oven. Bake for 1 hour, reducing the temperature if the water boils rapidly. The internal temperature of the stuffing should reach 160 degrees. Remove from the oven.

Monsieur François's hint to the home cook: The chestnuts will explode in the oven if an incision is not made through the shell before heating. Carefully follow the instruction on page 147.

Use 1½ pounds of your favorite mild breakfast sausage, in place of the pork and veal.

Faisan Rôti au Chou

Roast Pheasant with White Cabbage

Serves 4

2 young pheasants, 2 to 2½ pounds each
8 strips bacon
Salt and freshly ground pepper
3 tablespoons oil
¼ cup diced carrots
½ cup minced onions
½ cup chicken stock (page 115)
Braised white cabbage (page 155)

Preheat oven to 400 degrees.

Salt and pepper the pheasants inside and out. Lay 2 strips of bacon across the breasts of each bird. Truss the legs and wings, looping the string over the breasts to attach the bacon.

Place a roasting pan that will comfortably hold the birds on the stove. Add the oil and heat over medium high flame. When the oil begins to smoke, add the pheasants and brown them evenly, turning from time to time. Roast in the oven for 20 minutes, basting occasionally. Add the carrots and onions and cook for 10 to 15 more minutes. Test for doneness by pricking the breast with a fork. If the juice runs clear, the bird is cooked.

Brown the remaining four slices of bacon in a small pan and set aside.

Remove pan from the oven and set the pheasants aside. Pour the grease out of the pan, return it to the stove, and deglaze with the chicken stock.

Bring to a boil over high heat, scraping the bottom of the pan to dissolve any caramelized juices. Transfer the liquid to a small saucepan. Skim off any fat, taste, and adjust seasonings.

Remove the string and split the pheasants in half with a large heavy knife. Place on a warm platter garnished with the cabbage and bacon strips. Serve with the sauce.

Monsieur François's hints to the home cook: Only hunters and their friends know the taste of real wild game because of the requirement that all meat be federally inspected. The venison served in restaurants and sold in specialty stores is raised on game farms. Farm-raised game is readily available and is generally very tasty. The meat is of high quality from young animals, eliminating the problem of cooking old tough game. Whether the game is hunted or purchased, game dishes are among my favorites.

Salmis de Pintade de L'Auberge

Stewed Guinea Hens Hungarian Style

Serves 4

2 guinea hens, approximately 2 pounds each
Salt and pepper
2 teaspoons mild Hungarian paprika
Flour
2 tablespoons butter
¼ pound bacon cut into ¼-by-1 ½-inch strips (i.e., about ⅓ cup *lardons*)
⅓ cup finely chopped onions
1 green pepper, skin removed and diced (⅓ cup)
2 cups quartered fresh white mushrooms
1 cup dry white wine
⅓ cup sour cream
Pinch of minced garlic
Salt and pepper to taste

Stock:
2 tablespoons oil
Reserved bones from guinea hens
½ cup finely sliced onions
¼ cup finely sliced carrots
2 tablespoons flour
2½ cups cold water
1 *bouquet garni* consisting of 1 bay leaf, 4 sprigs parsley, 2 pieces celery
   stems, a pinch of thyme, and ¼ teaspoon cracked black peppercorns
   (see hint on page 4), wrapped in cheesecloth

Cut each bird into quarters with wings and breasts and legs and thighs attached. Remove the breast bones and the wing tips. Refrigerate the guinea hen quarters.

To prepare the stock, heat the oil in a heavy saucepan over high heat. Add the carcasses, necks, and gizzards and sauté for 10 minutes, stirring often. Add the onions and carrots and cook an additional 5 minutes. Dust the bones with flour and mix thoroughly. Cover the bones with the cold water, stirring vigorously and scraping the bottom of the pan to loosen the caramelized juices. Bring to a boil, skim thoroughly, add the *bouquet garni*, and boil gently for 45 minutes. Strain into a clean saucepan and spoon off any surface fat; approximately 1 cup of liquid should remain.

To prepare the hens, season the reserved quarters with salt and pepper, dust with 1 ½ teaspoons paprika, and dredge them in flour, shaking off any excess.

Melt the butter in a large saucepan, add the *lardons* and sauté. When the *lardons* are browned, lift them out with a slotted spoon and reserve. Add the prepared pieces of guinea hen and brown well on all sides. Remove the pieces from the pan. Add the onions and simmer until translucent. Return the *lardons* with the diced green pepper, quartered mushrooms, the remaining ½ teaspoon paprika and guinea hen pieces to the pan. Deglaze with the white wine and bring to a boil. Add the 1 cup of stock, cover and simmer until the hens are tender, 12 to 15 minutes.

Stir the sour cream into the sauce. Add the minced garlic and salt and pepper to taste.

Serve with spätzle (page 163).

Monsieur François's hint to the home cook: Pheasants may be prepared in the same manner. Omit the paprika and sour cream and you have a *salmis de faisan,* stewed pheasants.

Cailles aux Raisins et Baies de Genièvre

Quail with Grapes and Juniper Berries

Serves 4

8 quail
Salt and freshly ground pepper
4 tablespoons plus 5 tablespoons butter
8 pieces of fatback (2 by 2 by ⅛ inches)
2 tablespoons oil
1 cup seedless white grapes
1 teaspoon sugar

Sauce:

12 juniper berries, crushed and very finely chopped (approximately
   ¾ teaspoon)
2 teaspoons gin
1 cup chicken stock (page 115)
1 tablespoon butter

Crush and finely chop the juniper berries and macerate in the gin in a small bowl. Reserve for the sauce.

Preheat the oven to 400 degrees.

Season each bird inside and out with salt and pepper. Place ½ teaspoon of butter inside each bird. Lay a slice of fatback over the breast of each. Truss the birds, securing the fatback to the body.

In a large sauté pan, melt 2 tablespoons of the butter and the oil. When the butter begins to brown, place the birds breast side down in the pan and sear on all sides. Place the pan in the oven and roast about 12 minutes, turning each quail twice.

In another sauté pan, melt 2 more tablespoons of butter, add the grapes, and sprinkle with the sugar. Sauté 3 to 4 minutes, tossing often, and set aside.

Remove the quail from the oven, cut away the string from the birds, set aside, and keep warm.

Make the sauce by pouring off the grease from the roasting pan and deglazing with the chicken stock. Bring to a boil and transfer the liquid to a small saucepan. Add the gin and the berries. Remove from the heat, stir in the 1 tablespoon butter with a whisk, taste, and adjust seasonings.

Put two birds on each plate, garnish with the grapes, and set in the oven for 3 to 4 minutes to thoroughly heat.

Remove the plates from the oven. Pour the sauce around the birds. Serve with wild rice (page 161) and sautéed wild mushrooms (page 151).

Monsieur François's hint to the home cook: Juniper berries may be difficult to find. Try ordering them from an institutional grocery purveyor.

Cailles Farcies à notre façon

Stuffed Quail

Serves 4

8 partially boneless quail
Salt and pepper
3 tablespoons butter
2 tablespoons oil
1 cup chicken stock (page 115) or white stock (page 42).

Stuffing:
10 ounces duck meat with fat (use the legs and thighs left from duck
    breasts with apples and plums, page 117)
¾ teaspoon salt
Pinch of pepper
Pinch of pâté spices (page 20)
2 whole eggs
½ cup heavy cream

To prepare the stuffing, cut the duck meat with fat into small pieces and finely grind in a food processor fitted with the steel blade. Add the seasonings and eggs, blending thoroughly. Slowly pour the cream through the feed tube with the motor running until completely incorporated. Taste for seasonings and chill.

Preheat oven to 400 degrees.

Use a piece of kitchen twine to tie off the neck opening and season the inside of each quail with salt and pepper. Fill a pastry bag with the prepared duck meat and stuff the quail, dividing the stuffing evenly among the eight birds. Bend the legs forward against the body and tie together securely, completely enclosing the quail cavity.

Melt 2 tablespoons of the butter and oil in a large skillet over high heat. When the butter browns, add the quail and sear lightly on all sides. Place in the oven and roast for 15 minutes. Remove the quail from the oven, cut away the string. Set the quail aside and keep warm.

To prepare the sauce, pour the grease from the roasting pan and deglaze with the chicken stock. Bring to a boil and transfer the liquid to a small saucepan. Boil again, skim thoroughly, and remove from the heat. Whisk in 1 tablespoon of butter, taste, and adjust seasonings.

Place the quail, two per serving, on toast points on warm dinner plates. Pour the sauce around the birds and serve with wild rice (see page 161).

Monsieur François's hint to the home cook: We often serve the quail with a stuffing made exactly like the *farce aux marrons* (page 120), but without the chestnuts. Partly boneless quail are commercially available in gourmet markets or from institutional poultry purveyors.

Season the sauce with a tablespoon of sherry or Madeira.

Le Lapereau Rôti Farci aux Herbes de Provence

Roast Rabbit with Herb Stuffing

Serves 8

2 3- to 3½-pound rabbits
2½ tablespoons white wine
2 tablespoons dry mustard
Salt and freshly ground pepper
Kitchen twine
4 tablespoon butter
2 tablespoons oil

Sauce:
2 rabbit carcasses
1 tablespoon oil
½ cup chopped onions
½ cup chopped carrots
1½ tablespoons all-purpose flour
¼ cup white wine
5 cups water
2 bay leaves
4 cloves
1 tablespoon tomato purée
¼ teaspoon minced garlic
¼ teaspoon cracked black
  peppercorns (see hint on
  page 4)
¼ teaspoon thyme
Salt to taste

Stuffing:
1 cup minced onions
1 cup minced leeks
4 tablespoons butter
8 tablespoons *duxelles*
  (page 159)
4 tablespoons plain bread crumbs
1 teaspoon salt
¼ teaspoon freshly ground pepper
1 tablespoon minced shallots
1 teaspoons *herbes de Provence*,
  finely ground (see hint p. 127)
Salt to taste

Separate the front and hind legs at the joint next to the body. Remove the thigh bones from the hind legs at the second joint. Place each rabbit on its back with the neck opening away from you. Using a small, very sharp boning or paring knife, debone the loins, keeping them as intact as possible. Rest the blade of the knife against the surface of the bones and follow the rib cage downward on each side to the spine. When you reach the backbone, carefully slide the knife between the spine and the skin, leaving the loins attached. Reserve the rabbits in the refrigerator and prepare the sauce with the bones.

Heat oven to 400 degrees.

To make the sauce, cut the carcasses into four or five pieces with a heavy knife or cleaver. Heat the oil in a shallow baking pan or large skillet over high heat and brown the bones, stirring occasionally. When the bones are well browned, add the onions and carrots and place the pan in the oven for 30 minutes, turning the bones once or twice.

126

Remove the pan from the oven and drain off any fat. Mix the flour with the bones and vegetables and return the pan to the oven for 10 minutes more.

Transfer the contents of the pan to a large saucepan. Deglaze the roasting pan with the white wine, scraping the bottom to loosen any particles of meat. Pour the wine over the rabbit bones and add all the remaining ingredients except the salt. Bring to a full boil, reduce heat and simmer uncovered for 1 hour. The liquid should be reduced by half.

Strain through a chinois or fine sieve. Taste for seasoning and add salt to taste. Keep warm until time to serve.

To prepare the stuffing (you can do this while the sauce is cooking), melt 2 tablespoons of butter in a small saucepan. Cook the chopped onions until they are very soft and translucent, stirring often. Do not brown. Transfer the onions to a mixing bowl, wipe out the pan, and repeat with the leeks, cooking about 10 minutes.

Thoroughly mix all the ingredients together.

To assemble and cook the rabbits, mix the white wine and dry mustard together in a small bowl to form a paste.

Lay the rabbits out skin side down. Trim some of the skin from the edges to patch any torn areas between the loins.

Brush the loins and the inside of the thighs with the mustard and season with salt and pepper. Divide the stuffing between the two sets of loins and the four thighs. Fold the skin on one side, then the other, over the loins. Truss the stuffed loins and thighs securely with kitchen twine. Season the forelegs with salt and pepper.

Melt the butter and oil over high heat in a small roasting pan. When the butter begins to brown, carefully add the rabbit parts and sear on all sides. (Some of the stuffing invariably comes out, so do not be concerned.) Transfer the pan to the preheated oven. The front legs will require 12 minutes, the hind legs 17 mintues, and the rolled loins 25 minutes. A fork should easily pierce the flesh when the meat is ready. Remove the pieces as soon as they are done and reserve.

To serve, remove the string. Carve the loins and thighs in 1/4-inch diagonal slices. Cut the forelegs in half at the second joint.

Divide the slices and arrange in an overlapping manner with 1 piece of foreleg per plate. Heat in the oven for 2 to 3 minutes. Pour the sauce around the meat and serve with wild rice (page 161) and wilted spinach (page 152).

Monsieur François's hint to the home cook: *Herbes de Provence,* a combination of thyme, basil, rosemary, lavender, and fennel, may be purchased in fine food stores, or substitute equal portions of ground thyme, rosemary, and basil.

Les Escalopes de Chevreuil

Deer Scallopini with Roebuck Sauce

Serves 6

1 top or bottom round from a leg of deer, 2 to 3 pounds
Salt and pepper
2 tablespoons butter
1 tablespoon oil
2 cups roebuck sauce

Marinade:
1 onion, peeled and thinly sliced
1 carrot, thinly sliced
3 sprigs parsley
2 shallots, thinly sliced
Pinch of thyme
2 bay leaves
3 cloves
1 tablespoon red wine vinegar
¼ teaspoon cracked black peppercorns (see hint on page 4)
4 crushed juniper berries
1 clove garlic, peeled and crushed
3 cups strong red wine

Roebuck sauce:
2 tablespoons oil
2 tablespoons finely minced onion
2 tablespoons finely diced country ham
½ cup dry white wine
2 tablespoons red wine vinegar
1 quart basic deer sauce (page 45)
3 tablespoons red currant jelly
¾ tablespoon salt
¼ teaspoon freshly ground pepper

Four to five days before serving, separate the top or bottom round from a leg of deer and remove the silver skin. Reserve the bones and trimmings to make the deer sauce.

Combine the marinade ingredients in a bowl just large enough to accommodate the meat and the marinade. If the bowl is too large, extra wine will be needed. The deer should be completely covered with the marinade. Cover and store in the refrigerator, turning the meat every day.

To prepare the sauce, heat the oil in a 2-quart saucepan. Add the onions and simmer for 5 minutes until translucent. Add the ham, stir well, and cook for 1 minute.

Add the wine and wine vinegar, boiling down until almost dry.

Pour in the deer sauce, bring to a full boil, reduce heat, and simmer 10 to 12 minutes.

Stir in the currant jelly and the salt and pepper. Taste and adjust seasonings. Set aside and keep warm.

To prepare the deer, remove the deer from the marinade. Cut 18 scallopini ¼ inch thick across the grain of the meat. Lightly pound the slices with the side of a meat cleaver and season with salt and pepper.

Heat 2 tablespoons butter and 1 tablespoon of oil together in a large heavy skillet. When the butter begins to brown, quickly sauté the deer scallopini (will require several batches) no more than 15 seconds per side. Overcooking toughens the meat.

Transfer the meat to a warm platter and drain off the fat from the skillet. Deglaze the pan with the roebuck sauce. Bring to a boil and pour over the deer.

Serve at once with a sautéed apple ring, filled with cranberry sauce (page 56) and a portion of chestnut purée (page 147).

Monsieur François's hint to the home cook: Save any excess deer scraps for the *terrine de gibier* (page 22). Large pieces of meat not suitable for scallopini may be cubed, marinated, and stewed like the *civet de marcassin* (page 132).

Cuissot de Marcassin
Sauce Poivrade

Roast Haunch of Boar

Procuring the game for the following recipe may be hazardous to your health. As a boy in Alsace, Papa often participated in wild boar hunts. The hunters' children were used as "beaters" to flush the animals out of the brush. They would walk through the forest banging sticks against tree trunks and shouting to drive the boars toward the waiting hunters. On one such hunt, the children cornered a large boar in front of a ravine. It turned and charged, forcing Papa to scramble up the nearest tree. He lived to tell the tale. I hope your hunt is less eventful.

Serves 8

1 leg of boar, approximately 3 to 5 pounds (trimmed)
⅓ cup rendered duck fat or oil
Salt and pepper

Marinade:
1 bottle dry red wine (or enough to cover the meat in a container just
    large enough to hold it)
1 teaspoon red wine vinegar
1 cup sliced onions
½ cup carrots
Square of cheesecloth containing 1 clove of garlic crushed, 2 bay leaves, 4
    cloves, a pinch of thyme, parsley stems, ½ teaspoon cracked black
    peppercorns (see hint on page 4), and 6 to 8 crushed juniper berries

Stock:
Bones (cracked) and the trimmings from the leg of boar
1 tablespoon oil
Reserved vegetables from the marinade
3 tablespoons flour
5 cups cold water

Sauce:
⅓ cups red wine vinegar
1 teaspoon finely minced shallots
1¼ teaspoons cracked black peppercorns
2 cups boar stock
1 tablespoon butter
1 tablespoon port wine

Four to five days before serving, remove all but a ⅛-inch of fat from the surface of the leg and discard. Debone the haunch, except for the shank bone, removing the tail, hip, and leg bones. Trim away the meat around the top of the shank so that the exposed bone can be used as a handle when carving. Cover and reserve the bones and scraps in the refrigerator.

Combine all the marinade ingredients in a deep pan which is just large enough to hold the meat. Be sure the meat is completely covered with the marinade. Cover the pan and refrigerate. Turn the meat once a day.

To prepare the stock, begin 4 hours before serving. Preheat the oven to 500 degrees. Crack the bones with a cleaver and prepare the stock as follows.

Place the roasting pan in the oven for 10 minutes, then add the oil, followed by the bones and scraps. Brown the bones, stirring once or twice, for 30 minutes.

Lift the meat out of the marinade and drain completely in a colander. Strain the marinade into a bowl and set aside. Reserve the spice bag and add the drained marinated vegetables to the bones in the oven. Bake 15 more minutes. Dust the bones with the flour and cook an additional 5 minutes in the oven.

Remove the roasting pan from the oven and pour out as much fat as possible. Place the pan on top of the stove over high heat, add the 5 cups of cold water, and scrape the bottom of the pan to detach and dissolve the meat particles. Bring to a boil and transfer the entire contents along with the reserved spice bag to a stock pot. Boil again, skim thoroughly, reduce heat, and boil gently for about 1 ½ to 2 hours. Strain the stock into a bowl and skim off the surface fat; there should be approximately 2 cups of stock remaining. Reserve.

Clean the roasting pan.

Preheat the oven to 450 degrees.

Season the haunch generously inside and out with salt and pepper. Re-shape the leg and tie it with kitchen twine. Melt the oil or rendered duck fat in the roasting pan on top of the stove. Carefully place the boar in the hot oil and sear it on all sides. Set the pan in the oven and roast for 45 to 50 minutes, until the internal temperature reaches 140 to 150 degrees for medium. While the meat is roasting, finish the sauce.

To finish the sauce, combine the wine vinegar, shallots, and cracked peppercorns in a small saucepan. Bring to a boil and evaporate the liquid until almost dry. Add the reserved stock, and boil gently for 20 to 25 minutes. Strain into a saucepan, and stir in the butter and port wine with a whisk. Adjust seasonings. Cover and keep warm.

Remove the roast from the oven and allow the meat to rest 15 to 20 minutes and the juices to settle. Carve the meat across the grain and serve with the sauce, braised red cabbage (page 154), and cranberry sauce (page 56).

Monsieur François's hint to the home cook: Place the haunch in front of you on a cutting board, the shank bone pointing right, and remove the twine. Holding the meat in place with a fork, cut thin slices (¼ inch), working from left to right. Arrange the slices of boar on warm plates and serve with the sauce and garnishes.

Civet de Marcassin

Boar Stew

Serves 10

3½ to 4 pounds boar, shoulder and neck meat
5 tablespoons oil
1 cup *lardons* (bacon sliced into sticks ¼ inch thick and 1 inch long)
½ cup chopped onions
2 tablespoons flour
2 cups boar stock (page 124)
2 to 3 cups marinade
¼ teaspoon pâté spices (page 20)
1 tablespoon cognac
½ cup heavy cream
Salt and pepper

Marinade:
3 cups full-bodied red wine (approximately)
1 cup sliced onions
1 cup coarsely sliced carrots
1 tablespoon red wine vinegar
¼ teaspoon ground pepper
2 cloves
2 bay leaves
2 cloves garlic, peeled and crushed
Pinch of thyme

Cut the boar meat into 1-inch cubes and combine in a large bowl with all the marinade ingredients. Mix well, so that all the pieces of meat are coated with the marinade. Cover and refrigerate for 2 to 3 days.

Before preparing the stew, remove the meat from the marinade and drain well in a colander. Strain the liquid into a small saucepan. Bring to a boil, skim thoroughly, and reserve for use in the stew. Reserve the vegetables.

Preheat oven to 400 degrees.

Season the boar with salt and pepper. Heat 2 tablespoons of oil in a large skillet and sear half of the meat. Transfer the sautéd meat to a colander to drain. Add another 2 tablespoons of oil and brown the remaining meat on all sides and drain.

Heat the last tablespoon of oil in a large saucepan or a Dutch oven and sauté the *lardons* until lightly browned. Add the onions and cook until translucent, about 5 minutes.

Pour off the grease, add the meat to the Dutch oven, and place, uncovered, in the oven for 10 minutes, stirring once or twice.

Dust the meat with the flour and return to the oven for an additional 5 minutes. Mix the flour into the meat. Add the reserved vegetables and herbs from the marinade, the boar stock, and enough boiled marinade to completely cover the meat.

Cover the Dutch oven and set it in the oven. After 1 hour, reduce the heat to 325 degrees and continue cooking until the meat is easily pierced with a fork, approximately 2 more hours.

Remove the stew from the oven and skim thoroughly. Finish the sauce with the pâté spices, cognac, and cream. Taste and adjust seasonings. Serve with spätzle (page 163).

Monsieur François's hint to the home cook: Prepare the *civet* one or two days ahead. Set aside, reheat, and add the cream, cognac, and spices just before serving. Basic beef or veal sauce (page 39) may be substituted for the boar stock.

Les Salades

Salads

Vinaigrette Maison

Vinaigrette Dressing

Makes 2 cups

1 ½ cups soybean oil
¼ cup red wine vinegar
¼ cup tarragon vinegar
2 teaspoons finely minced onion
1 teaspoon finely minced shallots
¼ teaspoon finely minced garlic
2 teaspoons Dijon-style mustard
1 teaspoon dry mustard
½ teaspoon Worcestershire sauce
2 drops Tabasco sauce
¼ teaspoon chopped fresh tarragon
1 teaspoon salt
¼ teaspoon freshly ground pepper

Combine all the ingredients except the oil in a small bowl and beat together with a whisk until they are well blended.

Gradually beat in the oil. Taste and adjust seasonings.

Monsieur François's hint to the home cook: Add fresh herbs such as parsley and chives to taste. The vinaigrette naturally separates; be sure to shake well before using.

Different brands of mustards, vinegars and herbs will alter the final product. Adjust according to your preferences.

Salade de Mâche et Endives

Corn Salad and Belgian Endive

Serves 4

½ pound *mâche* (corn salad), approximately 1 quart
3 Belgian endives
3 scallions, finely minced
Freshly ground pepper
4 tablespoons croutons
½ pound lean bacon, diced
¼ cup vinaigrette (page 136)
2 eggs, hard boiled and chopped

Trim the roots, wash and dry the *mâche* leaves, and put them into the salad bowl. Wipe the 3 endives clean and separate the leaves directly into the bowl. Add the finely minced scallions and the croutons. Sprinkle with freshly ground pepper to taste.

Sauté the diced bacon until crisp and pour, with the fat included, over the salad. Add the vinaigrette. Quickly toss the salad and top with the chopped hard-boiled eggs. Serve at once.

Salade d'Haricots Verts

String Bean Salad

Serves 4

1 pound fresh string beans
1½ tablespoons finely minced onion
3 tablespoons vinaigrette (page 136)
¼ teaspoon salt
Pinch of freshly ground pepper

Snap off the tips and wash the beans. Bring 1 gallon of water with 4 tablespoons salt to a boil. Add the beans and cook 3 to 5 minutes, depending upon their size. They should remain crisp. Drain and plunge into a bowl of ice cold water.

Place beans in a colander, tossing occasionally to drain off all the water.

Mix the onion, vinaigrette, salt, and pepper in a bowl. Add the beans and toss gently. Taste for seasoning and serve.

Salade de Tomates Alsacienne

Alsatian-Style Tomato Salad

Serves 4

4 ripe tomatoes
1 head of Boston or Bibb lettuce
Salt and freshly ground black pepper
Pinch of sugar (optional, if tomatoes are not fully ripe)
4 tablespoons finely chopped onions
4 teaspoons finely minced scallions
2 teaspoons finely chopped fresh basil
2 teaspoons finely chopped fresh parsley
2 teaspoons red wine vinegar
4 tablespoons vinaigrette (page 136)

Wash the tomatoes and lettuce, drain both well. Make a bed of lettuce on four individual salad plates. Remove the stems and thinly slice the tomatoes. Fan out the tomatoes over the lettuce.

Season the tomatoes with a pinch of salt and pepper, and sugar, if desired. Top each tomato with 1 tablespoon onion, 1 teaspoon scallions, ½ teaspoon basil and ½ teaspoon parsley. Pour ½ teaspoon vinegar and 1 tablespoon vinaigrette over each serving.

Monsieur François's hint to the home cook: Use discolored or overripe tomatoes to prepare Tomato Bisque (page 11).

Salade de Gruyère

Swiss Cheese Salad

Serves 4

1 pound Gruyère cheese
3 rounded tablespoons finely chopped onions
2 tablespoons chopped parsley
⅓ cup vinaigrette (page 136)
Pinch salt and freshly ground pepper

Cut the cheese into medium julienne strips about 2 inches long.

Mix the vinaigrette, onion, parsley, salt, and pepper in a bowl. Add the cheese and toss well. Correct seasoning and serve.

Monsieur François's hint to the home cook: Serve alone as an appetizer or as a garnish with *charcuterie* (pâtés).

Salade de Concoubres

Cucumber Salad

Serves 4

1 to 2 cucumbers
¾ tablespoon salt
1 tablespoon Dijon-style mustard
½ cup vinaigrette (page 136)
Pinch freshly ground pepper
1 teaspoon finely chopped parsley

Peel the cucumbers and split them in half lengthwise. Scoop out the seeds with a small spoon. Thinly slice the cucumbers (⅛ inch thick). There should be 2 cups.

Place the cucumber slices in a colander and sprinkle with the salt. Toss once or twice to distribute the salt and let stand for about 1 hour. Rinse lightly with cold water and drain for a few minutes, tossing several times to remove more water.

In a small bowl thoroughly combine the other ingredients. Add the cucumber slices and toss well. Taste and adjust seasonings.

Salade de Betteraves

Beet Salad

Serves 4

3 to 4 medium beets
½ cup red wine vinegar
1 teaspoon sugar
6 cracked black peppercorns (see hint on page 4)
1 bay leaf
2 cloves
1 tablespoon peanut or soy oil
1 tablespoon onion, finely chopped
¼ teaspoon salt
1 pinch freshly ground pepper

Wash the beets and cut away the roots and stems. Cook the beets in salted boiling water for 35 to 40 minutes, or until they are tender. Beets are ready when a fork passes easily through the flesh.

When cool enough to handle, peel and cut the beets into a large julienne, ¼ by 1 inch. There should be approximately 2 cups. Place in a mixing bowl.

Combine the vinegar, sugar, peppercorns, bay leaf, and cloves in a small saucepan. Place over high heat, bring to a boil, and reduce by one third. Immediately strain this over the beets and add the oil, onion, salt, and pepper. Toss well and taste for seasoning.

Monsieur François's hint to the home cook: Serve as a garnish with pâté or as a salad.

Céleriac Rave Remoulade

Celery Root Salad

Serves 8

4 medium celery roots
1 cup mayonnaise (page 52)
1 ½ teaspoons dry mustard
⅛ teaspoon sugar
½ teaspoon lemon juice
¼ teaspoon salt
⅛ teaspoon freshly ground pepper
½ teaspoon parsley, finely chopped

Peel celery roots and cut into a julienne, the size of match sticks. In a bowl, mix mayonnaise with dry mustard, sugar, lemon juice, salt, and pepper. Gently toss the julienned celery roots with the remoulade sauce until well coated. Sprinkle the top with finely chopped parsley.

Monsieur François's hint to the home cook: Celery root or celeriac is found only during the fall and winter months.

Les Légumes et Accompagnements
Vegetables and Garnishes

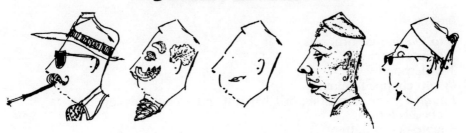

Purée de Brocoli

Broccoli Purée

Serves 4

2 to 2½ pounds broccoli
2 quarts water
1 tablespoon salt
⅓ cup chopped onions
Bouquet garni, consisting of 1 bay leaf and 2 cloves wrapped in
   cheesecloth
3 tablespoons butter
½ cup heavy whipping cream
2 tablespoons finely minced scallions
Salt and freshly ground pepper

Remove and discard the lower tough part of the broccoli stalks, reserving the flowerettes.

Bring the water, seasoned with the salt, to a full boil. Add the chopped onions and *bouquet garni*; simmer for 15 minutes. Add the broccoli and cook until tender, but still crisp, approximately 10 minutes.

Discard the *bouquet garni* and drain the broccoli in a fine sieve, reserving some of the liquid. Blend the broccoli and onions in a food processor, only enough to achieve a course purée. Mix in a small amount of liquid if the purée is too thick.

Return the mixture to the pot and reheat. Mix in the butter, cream, and scallions. Taste and adjust seasonings.

Monsieur François's hint to the home cook: The broccoli purée will turn yellow if heated excessively.

144

Purée Crécy

Carrot Purée
Our most popular vegetable

Serves 4

½ cup sliced onions
¼ cup diced leeks, washed well
2 tablespoons diced celery
1 *bouquet garni* consisting of 1 bay leaf and 2 cloves, wrapped in
  cheesecloth
1½ tablespoons salt
1 quart water
1 pound carrots, pared and sliced
2 scallions, very finely minced
2 tablespoons butter
½ cup heavy cream
Pinch of freshly grated nutmeg
Salt and freshly ground pepper

Combine the onions, leeks, celery, and *bouquet garni* in a saucepan with
the 1½ tablespoons salt and water. Bring to a boil and simmer for 10 to 15
minutes, until all the vegetables are tender.

Add the carrots and boil for approximately 15 minutes. Test with a fork
to be sure that the thickest part of the carrot can easily be pierced. Discard
the *bouquet garni* and drain the carrots, reserving ½ cup of the liquid.

Purée the carrots and vegetables in a blender or a food processor.
Return the purée to the pot and add the scallions, butter, cream, and
nutmeg. Reheat and season to taste. If the mixture is too thick, add some
of the reserved broth. Serve hot.

Monsieur François's hint to the home cook: Do not grind the
mixture too finely; some small vegetable chunks should remain.

Purée de Choux-Fleurs au gratin

Cauliflower Purée

Serves 4

1 medium-sized cauliflower, 1½ to 2 pounds
1 quart water
1 tablespoon salt
⅓ cup chopped onions
2 spring onions, very finely minced
6 tablespoons butter
½ cup heavy cream
Pinch of freshly grated nutmeg
Salt and pepper
½ cup of grated Gruyère cheese

Cut the cauliflower into flowerettes, discarding the tough center stem. Wash well and drain.

In a 2-quart saucepan, bring the salted water to a full boil. Add the onions and simmer for 15 minutes. Next, add the cauliflower and cook 6 to 10 minutes until flowerettes are tender, but still crisp. Drain the vegetables.

Preheat the broiler.

In a food processor, purée the cauliflower and onions together only enough to thoroughly blend the ingredients, which should retain a slightly coarse consistency.

Return the purée to the saucepan. Add the spring onions, 2 table-spoons of the butter, the cream, and the nutmeg. Mix well and season to taste.

Butter a 1-quart ovenproof dish with 2 tablespoons of the butter. Pour the cauliflower purée into the baking dish, top with the grated cheese, and dot with the 2 remaining tablespoons of butter. Place under the broiler until the cheese browns. Serve immediately.

Purée de Marrons

Chestnut Purée

Serves 6 to 8

2 pounds fresh chestnuts (4½ to 5 cups peeled chestnuts)
1 cup water
½ cup milk
¾ tablespoon butter
¼ cup heavy whipping cream
¼ teaspoon salt
Pinch of pepper
Pinch of sugar
½ teaspoon cognac

Preheat oven to 450 degrees.

With a small sharp knife, incise an X through the outside shell of each chestnut. Put chestnuts in shallow baking pan and place in oven for 10 minutes. Remove from heat. When cool enough to handle, remove outer shell and peel off the inside skin. The peeling process becomes more difficult as the chestnuts cool, so it may be necessary to reheat some of them.

Place chestnuts in a 2-quart saucepan. Cover with the water and milk, bring to a boil, and simmer 30 to 40 minutes or until the chestnuts are tender. Do not overcook. Drain. Purée in a food processor and return them to the saucepan. Stir in the butter and cream with a whisk. Season with salt, pepper, sugar, and cognac.

Serve.

Monsieur François's hint to the home cook: Whole chestnuts packed in water and tinned chestnut purée are available in fancy food stores.

Petits Pois à la Française

Peas in Cream

Serves 4

16 pearl onions, peeled (see hint on page 150)
2 cups shelled peas, approximately ¾ pound
1 small head of Boston lettuce
3 tablespoons butter
2 tablespoons finely minced onion
¾ cup heavy cream
⅓ teaspoon salt
Pinch of freshly ground pepper
Pinch of sugar

Boil 1 quart of water seasoned with 1 tablespoon of salt. Drop in the pearl onions and cook for 10 minutes, or until easily pierced with a fork. Lift out the onions with a slotted spoon and drain well.

In the same water, boil the peas for 4 to 6 minutes, depending on their size and freshness. Drain in a colander and rinse under cold water.

If you are fortunate enough to find extremely fresh and tiny *petit pois*, you may eliminate the above step.

Trim the outer leaves, rinse the head of lettuce, and shred with a sharp knife. (There should be about 1 cup of shredded lettuce.)

Melt the butter in the same pot in which the vegetables were just cooked. When the foam subsides, add the onions and cook over low heat 4 to 5 minutes, until translucent. Add the lettuce and wilt for 1 to 2 minutes. Pour in the cream and boil until thick enough to coat a spoon. This should take 3 to 4 minutes. Stir in the remaining salt, pepper, sugar, pearl onions, and peas. Heat thoroughly and serve.

Monsieur François's hint to the home cook: Overcooking destroys the delicate texture and flavor of the peas.

This is a fine dish even without the pearl onions.

Haricots Verts Sautés

Sautéed Fresh String Beans

After dinner at L'Auberge, patrons sometimes visit the kitchen to satisfy any questions concerning a certain recipe or to offer their compliments. In Papa's youth, mere oral expressions of gratitude were insufficient; an offering was required of all pilgrims seeking audience with the chef.

As custom demanded the guest was received and shown about the kitchen. The chef accepted his laurels graciously as befitting a leader. If, however, a refreshment had not arrived before the visitor turned to leave, it fell to the cooks to uphold the chef's honor. The *sous chef* would dust the apprentice's shoulders with flour (perfectly camouflaged on the white jacket) and send him on a holy sortie against the irreverent visitor. The apprentice would "accidentally" trip into the disrespectful one, speckling his garments and thereby avenging the discourtesy. A hearty laugh by all, an apology to the chef from the embarrassed guest, and the long awaited round of drinks invariably followed.

Serves 4

1 gallon cold water
4 tablespoons salt
1 pound small snap beans, well washed and tips removed
4 tablespoons butter
1 teaspoon finely minced shallots
Pinch of finely minced garlic
Large pinch of salt
Small pinch of freshly ground pepper
¼ teaspoon chopped fresh savory

Using a large deep pot, bring the gallon of salted water to a full boil. Then drop in the beans and cook until tender, but still quite crisp, about 4 to 5 minutes. Drain and immediately plunge the beans into a bowl of ice water to stop the cooking. Before sautéing, thoroughly drain the beans for at least 15 minutes in a colander.

Heat the butter in a medium skillet. When the butter begins to brown, add the beans and sauté them for approximately 2 minutes, tossing frequently. Add the shallots and garlic, and sauté with the beans for a few moments, tossing often.

Season with salt, pepper, and savory at the very last. Give a final toss and serve.

Monsieur François's hints to the home cook: Substitute your favorite fresh herb for the savory. If you use regular (large) beans, be sure to extend the cooking time, but keep them somewhat crisp.

Carottes et Petits Oignons glacés

Glazed Carrots and Onions

Serves 4

2 quarts water
2 tablespoons salt
1 pound pearl onions, peeled
1 pound carrots, pared and cut into ½-by-2-inch sticks
8 tablespoons butter
2 tablespoons granulated sugar
1 teaspoon minced shallots
Salt and pepper

Bring salted water to a boil in a 3-quart saucepan. Drop in the onions and cook them for 8 to 10 minutes. Do not overcook. The onions must remain slightly firm. Test by piercing an onion with a large fork. Lift the onions out of the pan with a slotted spoon and plunge into cold water.

In the same water used for the onions, boil the carrots for 5 to 7 minutes. Again, keep them slightly firm. After testing for doneness, plunge into cold water.

Drain well in a colander prior to sautéing.

Melt 4 tablespoons of the butter in a medium sauté pan. Add the onions and a pinch of salt. Cook over high heat, tossing once or twice. Then sprinkle with 1 tablespoon of the sugar. Keep tossing and cooking for 4 to 5 minutes or until the sugar is slightly caramelized. Add ½ teaspoon of the shallots and give a final toss or two to evenly distribute the shallots. Remove from the heat. Pour the onions into a bowl and keep them warm while you sauté the carrots.

Wipe out the small sauté pan used for the onions and repeat the same procedure for the carrots. Cover and keep warm until time to serve.

Monsieur François's hint to the home cook: Instead of peeling the pearl onions, drop them into boiling water for one minute and then transfer to cold water. The skins will slide right off.

Chanterelles Sautées

Sautéed Wild Mushrooms

Serves 4

1½ pounds fresh or 4 ounces dried chanterelles
3 tablespoons olive oil
Salt and freshly ground pepper
1 teaspoon finely minced shallots
¼ teaspoon finely minced garlic
1 teaspoon freshly chopped parsley

If using dried mushrooms, soak them in cold water for 24 hours. The water should be changed twice.

Wash either the fresh or the dried mushrooms in cold water several times. Be sure to lift the mushrooms out of the water, leaving the grit behind. Examine each mushroom, removing any dirt from the base of the stem. Drain the mushrooms well in a colander.

Heat the oil in a large skillet and add the mushrooms. Sauté the mushrooms 4 to 5 minutes, tossing frequently. Add the shallots, garlic, salt, and pepper. Toss two or three times. Sprinkle with the chopped parsley, give a final toss, and remove from the heat.

Monsieur François's hint to the home cook: See note with *Feuilleté de Chanterelles* on page 27.

Pois Gourmands Sautés

Sautéed Sugar Snap Peas

Serves 4

2 to 2½ cups prepared fresh sugar snap peas (approximately ⅔ pound)
2 tablespoons butter
Salt and pepper

Remove the strings from both sides of each pod. Wash the pods in cold water and drain thoroughly.

Melt the butter in a medium pan over moderate heat. Just as the butter begins to brown, add the peas. Cook for 2 to 3 minutes, tossing frequently.

Season with salt and pepper to taste and serve at once.

Monsieur François's hint to the home cook: Prepare snow peas in the same manner.

Pommes de Terre Sautées Lyonnaise

Sautéed Potatoes with Scallions
French Style Home Fries with a *Nouvelle* Twist

Serves 4

1½ pounds (approximately 4 medium) potatoes
3 tablespoons vegetable oil or rendered duck fat
1½ tablespoons butter
3 scallions, finely minced
Salt and pepper to taste

Wash potatoes. Place unpeeled in a 2-quart saucepan and cover with cold water. Bring to a boil, reduce heat, and simmer about 15 minutes. Potatoes must be only partly cooked. Test for doneness by piercing potatoes with a large meat fork. The fork should meet with some resistance. Cool the potatoes under cold running water.

Peel the potatoes, cut them in half, and then into slices ¼ inch thick.

Heat the oil and butter in a heavy skillet. When the butter begins to brown, add the potato slices. Cook the potatoes until well browned and crisp, tossing frequently, approximately 5 minutes.

Add the scallions, a pinch of salt and pepper. Toss and serve.

Epinards Fondus

Wilted Spinach

Serves 4

12 ounces fresh spinach leaves
2 tablespoons butter
1 teaspoon minced shallots
Salt and freshly ground pepper

Discard any discolored leaves and remove the stems from the spinach. Wash the leaves in several changes of cold water. Lift the spinach out of the water, leaving the dirt behind.

Drain well in a colander.

Melt the butter in a large sauté pan, but do not brown. Add the shallots, cook for 10 seconds, and immediately add the spinach. Season with salt and pepper. Sauté 2 to 3 minutes, tossing frequently until spinach wilts. Serve hot.

Monsieur François's finishing touch: Add a pinch of ground nutmeg just before removing the spinach from the pan.

Chou-Fleur Polonaise

Cauliflower Polonaise

Serves 6

2 heads cauliflower
1 stick butter
1 teaspoon chopped garlic
½ cup plain bread crumbs
½ teaspoon *herbes de Provence* (see note on page 127)
¼ teaspoon salt
Pinch of freshly ground pepper
2 tablespoons chopped parsley
1½ tablespoons red wine vinegar
1 hard-boiled egg

Remove the outer leaves and the center stem from each cauliflower. Separate them into flowerettes.

Bring 2 quarts of water and 2 tablespoons of salt to a full boil. Add the flowerettes and cook approximately 12 minutes. The cauliflower should be tender but still crisp. Drain in a colander.

Preheat oven to 350 degrees.

Melt ½ stick of the butter in a small saucepan. Add the garlic and quickly mix in the bread crumbs, herbs, and salt and pepper. Combine very well and remove from the heat. Stir in 1 tablespoon parsley.

Brown the remaining butter.

Place the flowerettes in an ovenproof serving dish just large enough to hold them closely together. Sprinkle with wine vinegar and moisten with the browned butter. Coat with the bread crumb mixture and bake for 10 minutes.

Chop the egg and combine with the remaining parsley. Remove the cauliflower from the oven and sprinkle with chopped egg mixture. Serve very hot.

Chou Rouge Braisé

Braised Red Cabbage

When Papa was an apprentice in Alsace's Hôtel Chambard, *le patron* was loath to discard anything, and he found profitable uses for the seemingly most worthless materials. As an apprentice, Papa not only cleaned the ovens but also disposed of the dining room fireplace ashes. After cleaning the hearth, he was sometimes sent, bucket of ashes in hand, to the cellar and instructed to "dust" the bottles. In those days the labeling and dating of wine was not as strictly controlled as today. Many wines arrived in barrels and were bottled right in the restaurant's cellar. So Papa tossed a few handfuls of ashes over the racked bottles, thereby "aging the wine." The thick layer of dust on the bottles gave the impression of years of cellaring, naturally impressing the customers and enhancing their enjoyment, not to mention the price of the wine.

Serves 6

2 medium-sized red cabbages
1 teaspoon salt
Pinch of freshly ground pepper
1/3 cup red wine vinegar
2 apples
1/4 pound bacon, diced
2 cups slivered onions
Pinch of sugar
1 *bouquet garni* consisting of 2 bay leaves, 3 cloves, and
    1/4 teaspoon cracked black peppercorns (see hint on page 4),
    wrapped in cheesecloth
1 cup red wine
1/4 teaspoon minced garlic

Remove the tough outer leaves from the cabbages. Cut each into quarters and rinse under cold water. Remove the center core and cut the quarters into large juliennes. Place the cabbage in a large bowl and season with salt, pepper, and wine vinegar. Toss well and set aside (overnight if you wish).

Preheat oven to 375 degrees.

Peel, quarter, and dice the apples.

Place a deep flameproof baking pan on the stove over a moderate heat and add the diced bacon. Cook for several minutes until the bacon begins to brown. Add the onions and sweat for five minutes, stirring often. Add the apples, cabbage, and any liquid in the bowl to the baking pan, along with the sugar, *bouquet garni*, and red wine. Mix the ingredients thoroughly, cover the pan, and bake in the oven for 35 to 40 minutres. The cabbage should remain slightly crisp.

Remove from the oven, discard the *bouquet garni*, add the garlic, and adjust seasonings.

Monsieur François's hint to the home cook: The cabbage may be prepared ahead of time and reheated.

Chartreuse de Choux

Braised White Cabbage

Serves 6

2 white cabbages
4 tablespoons rendered goose fat or oil
¼ pound bacon, diced
2 cups slivered onions
2 cups thinly sliced carrots
1 cup white wine
1 *bouquet garni* consisting of 2 bay leaves, 3 cloves, and
 ¼ teaspoon cracked black peppercorns (see hint on page 4),
 wrapped in cheesecloth
1 teaspoon salt
Pinch of freshly ground pepper

Trim the tough outer leaves and cut the cabbages into quarters. Rinse under cold water. Remove the center stem and slice the quarters into thick juliennes.

Preheat oven to 375 degrees.

Melt the fat in a flameproof casserole and sauté the bacon until the pieces begin to brown. Mix in the onions and carrots and sweat for 5 minutes, stirring once or twice.

Stir in the cabbage, white wine, *bouquet garni*, and seasoning. Cover the casserole and place in the oven. Bake for 30 to 40 minutes, stirring occasionally, until the cabbage is tender. Do not overcook.

Remove from the oven and adjust the seasonings.

Monsieur François's hint to the home cook: The cabbage should remain slightly crisp, especially if prepared ahead and reheated.

Courgettes Niçoise

Zucchini and Yellow Squash with Tomato and Basil

If your guests balk at even trying the squash, tell them what Frieda Bene, Monsieur François's right arm in the dining room, says: "No dessert, if you don't finish your vegetables." It works every time.

Serves 4

Sauce:
1 tablespoon olive oil
1 tablespoon finely diced bacon
½ cup shredded onions
½ cup dry white wine
1 cup water
2 plum tomatoes, peeled and chopped (about 4 tablespoons)
⅓ cup diced green pepper
3 tablespoons tomato purée
1 tablespoon sugar (optional)
1 rounded tablespoon finely chopped garlic
1½ teaspoon salt
¼ teaspoon pepper
⅓ teaspoon freshly chopped basil

Vegetables:
2 cups sliced zucchini rounds, ⅛ inch thick
2 cups sliced yellow squash rounds, ⅛ inch thick
Salt and pepper
4 tablespoons olive oil

Heat the olive oil in a heavy saucepan. Sauté the bacon in the oil until the bits begin to brown. Add the onions and cook, stirring often until translucent, about 5 minutes. Pour in the wine and bring to a boil. Stir in all the remaining ingredients, except the basil. Boil gently for 15 minutes.

While the sauce is cooking, prepare the squash and zucchini. Heat two tablespoons of the olive oil in a large sauté pan. Add the zucchini, salt, and pepper, and sauté, tossing frequently, for about 3 to 4 minutes. Lightly color, but do not scorch. Transfer the zucchini to a colander, drain, and discard any burned pieces. Repeat with the yellow squash.

Stir the squashes into the sauce. Cover and simmer for 10 minutes, shaking the pan occasionally. The squash should be tender, yet slightly crisp. Remove from the heat, stir in the basil, and adjust the seasonings.

Monsieur François's hint to the home cook: This dish may be prepared ahead of time and reheated.

Tomates Provençale

Baked Tomatoes with Herbs

Serves 6

2 tablespoons butter
1 teaspoon finely minced garlic
½ cup plain bread crumbs
¼ teaspoon salt
Pinch of freshly ground pepper
½ teaspoon of combined ground rosemary, thyme, and bay leaf, or
    herbes de Provence (see note on page 127)
1 tablespoon freshly chopped parsley
6 ripe medium tomatoes
Salt and freshly ground pepper
Olive oil

Melt butter in a small saucepan. Add the garlic and cook 5 seconds. Immediately mix in the bread crumbs, salt, pepper, spices, and parsley. Thoroughly blend in the ingredients, with a large spoon and remove from the heat.

Preheat oven to 400 degrees.

Wash and dry the tomatoes. Remove the stems with a small knife and cut each tomato in half, crosswise. Brush with a little olive oil, season with salt and pepper, and place in a baking pan. Bake the tomatoes approximately 8 to 10 minutes, only enough to heat them thoroughly. Cooking time will vary, depending upon the ripeness of the tomatoes. Remove from oven.

Increase oven temperature to broil.

When ready to serve the tomatoes, generously sprinkle each half with seasoned bread crumbs. Brown lightly under the broiler and serve.

Tomates-Concassées

Cooked Tomatoes

Makes 1¼ cups

2 pounds ripe tomatoes
1 tablespoon olive oil
2 tablespoons finely minced onion
2 tablespoons tomato purée
Pinch of finely minced garlic
1 bay leaf
1 clove
Salt and freshly ground pepper

Bring two quarts of water to a boil and add the tomatoes for 10 to 20 seconds. Lift the tomatoes out of the water with a slotted spoon and drop them into a bowl of cold water. Cool the tomatoes a few moments and remove from the water. Peel off the skin and remove the stems. Slice the tomatoes in half, and place them in a large-holed collander set over a bowl. Press the tomato halves to force out the juice and seeds. Coarsely chop the tomato pulp (there should be approximately 2 cups) and set aside.

Heat the oil in a medium-sized skillet, add the onions, and sweat over low heat for about 5 minutes, until translucent. Stir in the chopped tomatoes, the tomato purée, and the remaining ingredients. Simmer over low heat for approximately 15 minutes, allowing the mixture to reduce and thicken. Remove the bay leaf and clove. Cool, cover and store in the refrigerator.

Monsieur Francois's hint to the home cook: Use whole canned tomatoes in the off-season. Use the remaining tomato juice in a soup or a stock.

Croutons

Makes 2 cups

½ stick butter
¼ cup vegetable oil
2 cups cubed bread, with crusts removed
Salt

Heat the butter with the oil in a sauté pan over a moderate flame. When the butter begins to brown, add the cubes and toss well, allowing them to brown evenly. Keep the cubes moving in the pan so they do not burn. Pour the croutons into a colander and salt them lightly. Drain to remove any excess oil.

Monsieur François's hint to the home cook: It is important that the butter/oil combination be very hot, so that the pieces of bread will toast quickly, rather than absorb the grease. The finished product should always be crusty, not filled with oil. Croutons are simply not as good the next day.

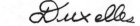

Cooked Chopped Mushrooms

Makes 2 cups

3 tablespoons butter
1 pound mushrooms, finely chopped
3 tablespoons finely minced shallots
½ teaspoon lemon juice
½ teaspoon salt
¼ teaspoon freshly ground pepper
2 tablespoons heavy whipping cream.

In a medium saucepan, melt the butter, add the mushrooms, shallots, and lemon juice, and reduce over high heat until mushroom moisture evaporates. Add salt, pepper, and heavy cream and remove from heat.

Monsieur François's hint to the home cook: Keep the duxelles covered and refrigerated until ready to use.

Champignons à Blanc

Cooked Mushrooms for Garnish

Serves 4

1/3 pound fresh white mushrooms
1/4 cup water
1/4 teaspoon salt
1/4 cup dry white wine
1 tablespoon lemon juice
1 tablespoon butter

Detach the stems from the mushrooms and reserve stems for use in a stock. Wash the mushrooms in cold water twice, lifting them from the water so that the grit stays in the bottom of the bowl.

In a 2-quart saucepan combine the remaining ingredients. Bring to a boil. Add the mushrooms and stir them carefully, so that each mushroom is coated with some of the hot liquid. Cook the mushrooms for 3 to 4 minutes.

Remove from the heat and allow the mushrooms to remain in the broth until time to serve.

Monsieur François's hint to the home cook: Reheat the mushrooms in their own broth.

160

Riz Sauvage

Wild Rice

Papa had never encountered wild rice before coming to the United States. It was his Uncle Jacques who taught him to flavor the wild rice with onions.

Serves 6

1 cup wild rice
1 quart water
1 teaspoon salt
5 tablespoons butter
¾ cup finely chopped onions
Salt and freshly ground pepper

Place the rice in a fine strainer and rinse under cold running water.

Bring 1 quart of water with 1 teaspoon salt to a boil. Add the rice, reduce the heat, and simmer, partly covered, until tender, 35 to 40 minutes.

As soon as the rice is cooking, melt 3 tablespoons of the butter in a small heavy saucepan. Add the onions and cook slowly, stirring occasionally until golden brown, 15 to 20 minutes.

Drain and spread rice on a platter or small baking sheet. Dice the two remaining tablespoons of butter and gently fold into the rice along with the browned onions using a fork.

Taste and adjust seasonings.

Riz Pilaf

Rice Pilaf

Serves 6

5 tablespoons butter
4 tablespoons onion, finely chopped
1 cup long-grain rice
3 cloves
1 bay leaf
1 teaspoon salt
¼ teaspoon pepper
1½ cups *fonds blanc* (page 42) or chicken consommé

Preheat oven to 375 degrees.

In a 1-quart saucepan melt, but do not brown, 3 tablespoons of the butter. Add the onions and cook over low heat until translucent, about 5 minutes. Stir occasionally.

Pour in the rice, thoroughly mixing with the butter and onions. Add the cloves, bay leaves, salt, and pepper, and cover rice with *fonds blanc* to a level of ¼ inch above the rice. Bring to a boil, cover, and put in the oven for about 19 minutes, or until tender.

Remove from oven and spread rice on a platter or small baking pan. Dice the 2 remaining tablespoons of butter and gently fold into the rice with a fork. Correct seasonings and serve.

Spätzle

Alsatian-Style Noodles

Serves 4 to 6

1½ cups sifted all-purpose flour
¼ teaspoon salt
Pinch each of nutmeg and pepper
1 tablespoon chopped fresh parsley
2 whole eggs
⅛ cup water (approximately)
2 tablespoons butter

Place the flour in a large mixing bowl with the salt, nutmeg, pepper, and parsley.

Break the eggs into a small bowl and beat well with a fork. Gradually pour the eggs into the flour, mixing thoroughly with your hand or a flexible rubber spatula. Add the water a little at a time and mix until the dough no longer adheres to the sides of the bowl. The dough should be rather firm, the consistency of a thick batter.

Bring 2 quarts of water with 2 tablespoons of salt to a rapid boil. Cover the pot of water with a spätzle maker or a colander with large holes (¼ to ⅜ inch in diameter). Force the dough through the holes with the rubber spatula. Use about one-third of the dough at a time. Allow the spätzle to cook until they rise to the surface, about 3 to 5 minutes. Using a slotted spoon, transfer the cooked spätzle into a large bowl of cold water. Repeat until all the dough is used.

To serve, thoroughly drain the spätzle in a colander. Melt the butter in a skillet. When the butter begins to brown, add the spätzle and sauté for 1 to 2 minutes until hot. Season with salt and pepper and serve.

Monsieur François's hint to the home cook: Spätzle are easy to prepare and may be served in place of noodles, especially with meat or game dishes. If the batter is too stiff to comfortably push through the colander, add more water.

Gnocchi Florentine

Spinach Gnocchi

Serves 6 to 8

2 cups fresh spinach leaves
1 quart milk
¾ cup cream of wheat (regular)
4 egg yolks
1 tablespoon salt
¼ teaspoon freshly ground pepper
Large pinch of freshly grated nutmeg
3 tablespoons butter
¾ cup shredded Gruyère cheese

Remove the stems and wash the spinach in several changes of cold water. Finely chop the leaves and set aside.

Scald the milk in a 2-quart saucepan and stir in the cream of wheat. Cook over moderate heat for 4 to 5 minutes.

Preheat oven to 400 degrees.

Remove the pan from the heat and beat in the egg yolks with a whisk, one at a time, blending thoroughly. Stir in the chopped spinach, salt, pepper, and nutmeg.

Butter a small baking pan or au gratin dish with 2 tablespoons of the butter and pour in the batter. The batter should be about 1 inch deep in the pan. Cover with the shredded cheese, dot with the remaining butter, and bake until nicely browned, about 12 to 15 minutes.

Spoon onto warm dinner plates or serve directly from the baking dish.

Les Patisseries et Desserts

Pastry and Desserts

Pâte Brisée

Pie Crust

Makes one 9-inch tart

1 cup all-purpose flour
½ teaspoon salt
6 tablespoons (¾ stick) unsalted butter at room temperature
2 tablespoons cold water

Sift the flour and salt together in a mixing bowl. Cut the butter into small cubes. Make a well in the flour and place the butter cubes in the center. Using your fingertips, blend the butter into the flour until the dough is crumbly. Add the cold water and knead lightly, only long enough to mix the ingredients. Form the dough into a ball, wrap in plastic, and refrigerate a minimum of 2 hours, overnight if possible.

Roll out the dough on a floured work surface and press evenly into the pie pan. Chill for 1 hour before baking.

Preheat oven to 375 degrees.

Remove the pie pan from the refrigerator and prick bottom of the dough with a fork. There are various methods of preventing the dough from rising, such as weighting it with rice or beans. We prefer placing a second pan in the dough-lined pie pan, thereby sandwiching the dough between two molds.

Bake for 15 minutes, remove the top pan or beans, and cook another 10 minutes, or until light brown.

Monsieur François's hint to the home cook: The dough may be prepared a day ahead and stored tightly wrapped in the refrigerator.

Pâte Feuilletée

Puff Pastry

Makes 2½ pounds

1 pound unsalted butter
1 pound sifted pastry flour
1 ½ teaspoons salt
1 cup cold water

Remove the butter from the refrigerator and allow to soften slightly.

Measure out ⅔ cup flour and set aside.

Place the remaining flour and salt in a food processor fitted with the steel blade. Pour the cup of cold water in with the flour and turn on the machine for 3 to 4 seconds. Remove the lid and scrape the flour into the center of the bowl with a rubber spatula. Run the machine for another 2 to 3 seconds. Turn the soft dough out onto a floured work surface, scrape any clinging dough out of the bowl, and add to the main mass.

Place the ⅔ cup flour into the food processor. Cut the butter into ½-inch pieces and drop them into the machine. Turn on for 4 to 5 seconds. Stop the machine, scrape the butter to the center, and run another 3 to 4 seconds. Scrape the butter and flour mixture out of the machine and form it into a small square approximately 6 by 6 by 1 ½ inches. Refrigerate while rolling out the dough.

Roll the soft dough into a square about 12 by 12 by ½ inches. Remove the "bar" of butter from the refrigerator and place it in the center of the square. Fold the four corners over the butter as to completely encase it. Dust the top of the dough lightly with flour and roll into a long rectangle about 18 by 8 by ⅜ inches.

Roll from the center out to evenly distribute the butter. For an even dough, it is important that the work surface be properly floured during the rolling process. If at any point the butter seems too soft, refrigerate the dough for 30 minutes.

Fold the dough back on itself in three equal parts like a formal letter. Be sure to brush off any excess flour before and after each fold. Slide the dough around 90 degrees, so the open end is in front of you. Roll out into a rectangle and fold in letter fashion again.

Wrap the dough in plastic and refrigerate at least 1 hour before twice repeating the rolling and folding process. Chill for 1 more hour, roll, and fold the dough two more times for a total of six. Cover and refrigerate at least 1 hour, even overnight, before using. The puff dough may be frozen for later use, but make sure it is well wrapped.

Monsieur François's hint to the home cook: Making your own puff pastry, though time-consuming, is naturally the best way to go. However, the puff pastry that you can purchase at your favorite bakery may be quite acceptable.

Crème Pâtissière

Pastry Cream

Makes 1½ cups

1 cup milk
¼ vanilla bean (about 1 ½ inches long) or ¼ teaspoon pure vanilla extract
Twist each of lemon and orange rind
3 large egg yolks
⅓ cup plus 1 tablespoon sugar
1 tablespoon flour
1 tablespoon cornstarch

Combine the milk, vanilla bean, and lemon and orange twists, in a copper or stainless steel saucepan. Place over high heat and bring to a boil. Remove vanilla bean and twists.

Beat the egg yolks and ⅓ cup sugar together in a bowl until the mixture whitens, using a wire whisk or electric mixer. Stir in the flour and cornstarch, blending until smooth.

Slowly pour the hot milk into the egg yolk mixture, beating vigorously with a wire whisk. (If you are using vanilla extract instead of vanilla bean, add the extract now.)

Pour back into the saucepan, place over medium heat, and boil the mixture for 1 minute, stirring constantly to prevent the custard from sticking to the bottom of the pan.

Pour the pastry cream into a bowl and sprinkle with 1 tablespoon of sugar. This prevents the formation of skin on the surface. Allow to cool. Cover and refrigerate.

Monsieur François's hint to the home cook: Pastry cream may be flavored in numerous ways. Among our favorites are *les eaux-de-vie* fruit brandies, *kirsch* (cherry), and *framboise* (raspberry).

Biscuit de Savoie au Chocolat

Chocolate Sponge Cake

Makes one 10-inch cake

6 large eggs, separated
1⅔ cups sifted powdered sugar
4 tablespoons warm tap water
½ cup sifted cornstarch
⅓ cup sifted cake flour
3 tablespoons sifted powdered cocoa
Pinch of baking powder
¼ teaspoon pure vanilla extract
Pinch of salt

Separate the eggs, making sure that the whites are free of any yolk.

Preheat oven to 350 degrees.

Whip the yolks and 1 cup of the sugar at high speed for 5 minutes, until the mixture whitens and forms a ribbon. Reduce speed and fold in the water, cornstarch, cake flour, cocoa, baking powder, and vanilla. Set aside.

Whip the egg whites with the pinch of salt in a separate bowl. Beat at low speed; then increase speed while gradually adding the remaining ⅔ cup sugar. The whites should form soft peaks. Be careful not to overwhip.

Gently fold the whites into the yolk mixture with a large rubber spatula. Pour into a 3-inch deep well-buttered and floured 10-inch cake pan.

Bake in the preheated 350-degree oven for approximately 25 minutes. Test by inserting a skewer or toothpick into the cake; when it comes out clean, the cake is done.

Remove cake from the pan immediately and cool completely before using.

Monsieur François's hint to the home cook: To make a white sponge cake, add 3 tablespoons cake flour to the ⅓ cup cake flour; and omit the 3 tablespoons powdered cocoa.

Crème au Beurre au Chocolat

Chocolate Butter Cream

Makes one 3-layer 10-inch cake

3 large eggs
¾ cup powdered sugar
1 pound unsalted butter
8 ounces dark bittersweet chocolate
½ teaspoon vanilla
Pinch of salt
1 to 3 tablespoons dark rum (optional)

Combine the eggs and powdered sugar in a deep stainless steel bowl and beat with a wire whisk or electric beater on medium speed until the mixture whitens. Place the bowl in a boiling water bath and continue beating for 5 minutes until the mixture thickens to the consistency of a light hollandaise sauce. Remove from the water bath.

Melt the butter and chocolate together in a small heavy saucepan, stirring often to prevent scorching. Remove from the heat when completely melted and stir into the egg and sugar mixture. Add the vanilla and salt, and whip at high speed for 3 to 4 minutes. Chill the butter cream for approximately 15 minutes and then whip at high speed for 4 to 5 minutes until a smooth spreading consistency is reached. The butter cream will lighten in color and increase in volume during the final whisking.

Monsieur François's hints to the home cook: Flavor the butter cream with 1 to 2 tablespoons of dark rum, if desired. The butter cream may be prepared in advance. Refrigerate until 30 minutes before use, and beat for a few minutes to reconstitute the butter cream.

If the butter cream appears to curdle, briefly place over warm water. Remove from the heat and whip at high speed until smooth. If too soft, chill the butter cream, and then beat until smooth.

The butter cream may be flavored in any number of ways besides chocolate. You may use, for example, coffee or hazelnut.

If bittersweet chocolate is unavailable, mix 5 ounces of semisweet with 3 ounces of unsweetened chocolate.

Tarte aux Quetsches

Plum Pie

When discussing the many provincial cuisines of France, Papa says, with absolute conviction and objectivity, that Alsatian cooking is the greatest: "The food in the interior [what he calls the rest of France] cannot match it." Here is another recipe of Alsatian extraction. Judge for yourself.

Serves 6 to 8

1 9-inch pie crust (page 160)
2½ pounds small purple plums (Italian plums)
3 tablespoons graham cracker crumbs
4 to 6 tablespoons sugar
Cinnamon sugar (1 tablespoon sugar, plus ¼ teaspoon cinnamon)

Bake the pie crust in a 400-degree preheated oven until lightly browned, about 20 minutes.

Split the plums lengthwise with a sharp knife and remove the pits. Taste one of the plums to ascertain the sweetness of the fruit.

Spread the graham cracker crumbs in the bottom of the pie shell. Place the plum halves, skin side down, in tight concentric circles around the pie. Plums should be resting on one another at a slight angle.

Bake in the 400-degree oven for 30 to 40 minutes. The plums are cooked when the skins tear easily.

Remove from the oven and immediately dust with the 4 to 6 tablespoons sugar, depending on the tartness of the fruit, and the cinnamon sugar.

Serve warm. Although this pie is elegant served alone, it is often requested with one of our homemade ice creams.

Monsieur François's hint to the home cook: Italian plums are the closest to the real *quetsches*. They are in season from mid-August through September.

Tarte aux Pommes - Alsacienne

Alsatian-Style Apple Pie

How does one make a lowly *cuisine courante* dish into an outstanding French culinary marvel? Baptize it with booze, of course. One afternoon, at the downtown Chez François, a pan of baked apples was prepared for the staff. The apples were peeled, cored, and baked with butter and sugar until soft. One was served to Monsieur François for dessert. He enjoyed it very much and sure enough a "new" dessert appeared on the menu the following day. By sprinkling the apples with a little Kirsch after baking, and dabbing them with whipped cream before serving, *voilà, les pommes fourées alsacienne Chantilly"*.

You too can "frenchify" hundreds of *repas* with a little imagination and a shot or two of wine and spirits. What gall we French have!

Serves 6 to 8

1 9-inch pie crust (page 166)
4 apples, Golden Delicious or cooking apples
3 whole eggs
¾ cup granulated sugar
¾ cup milk
¼ cup table cream
½ teaspoon cinnamon
Pinch of nutmeg
1 teaspoon kirsch
Pinch of salt
4 tablespoons unsalted butter
Cinnamon sugar (1 teaspoon sugar plus ⅛ teaspoon cinnamon)

Bake the pie crust in a 400-degree preheated oven for about 20 minutes, or until light brown.

Peel, core, and cut each apple into eight sections.

Beat the eggs and ½ cup of the sugar together with a wire whisk. Add the milk, cream, cinnamon, nutmeg, kirsch, and salt. Brown 2 tablespoons of butter in a large skillet and add to the custard. Blend well and set aside.

Brown the remaining 2 tablespoons of butter; add the apple wedges and sprinkle with ¼ cup sugar. Cook over high heat, allowing the sugar to caramelize. Toss the apples occasionally.

Arrange the caramelized apple wedges in the pie shell and fill with the custard. Bake at 400 degrees until the custard is set, approximately 20 minutes.

A knife inserted into the center of the custard should come out clean. Remove from the oven and dust with the cinnamon sugar. Serve warm.

Monsieur François's hint to the home cook: Prepare the tart using pears in place of the apples.

Tarte aux Pommes Weber

Honey Glazed Apple Tart

This recipe was given to me by M. Joseph Weber,
Patisserie Alsacienne, Paris.

Serves 6–8
1 9-inch pie crust (see page 166)
3 large Golden Delicious apples
2 tablespoons butter
3 tablespoons sugar

Custard:
2 medium eggs
⅓ cup sugar
4 level tablespoons all-purpose flour
¾ cup milk
¾ cup heavy whipping cream
½ teaspoon vanilla extract

Honey Glaze:
½ stick unsalted butter
3½ tablespoons sugar
3 tablespoons honey
3 tablespoons heavy whipping cream
½ cup blanched sliced almonds
2 rounded tablespoons raisins

Bake the pie crust in a 400 degree preheated oven for about 20 minutes,
or until light brown.

Peel, core, and cut each apple into six sections.

Brown the 2 tablespoons of butter in a large sauté pan over high
heat, add the apple wedges, toss to coat with butter, and sprinkle with
the 3 tablespoons of sugar. Cook for 2 or 3 minutes over high heat,
allowing the sugar to caramelize onto the apple wedges. Toss the apples
occasionally. Set aside.

Preheat the oven to 375 degrees.

To prepare the custard, use a wire whisk to cream the eggs and
sugar together in a stainless steel or glass bowl. Thoroughly blend in the
flour and add the cream, milk, and vanilla extract. Blend well and set
aside.

Arrange the caramelized apple wedges in concentric circles in the
pie shell and fill with custard. Bake at 375 degrees until the custard is set,
approximately 25 minutes. While the pie is baking, assemble the honey
glaze ingredients, but do not cook until the pie is removed from the oven.

To prepare the honey glaze, combine the butter, sugar, honey, and
cream in a small heavy saucepan and bring to a boil over high heat. Boil
rapidly until the mixture thickens and coats a spoon (210 degrees on a

candy thermometer). Remove from the heat and immediately stir in the raisins and almonds. Pour the glaze over the baked apple pie, spreading evenly with a spatula.

Return the pie to the oven and bake for approximately 10 minutes, until the almonds turn a golden brown.

Serve warm.

Monsieur François's hint to the home cook: we prefer Golden Delicious apples to other so-called cooking apples.

Tarte aux Paires

Pear Tart

Serves 10

1 cup granulated sugar
2 cups water
11 medium pears
1 11-inch pie pan with removable bottom
½ of the recipe for *Les Sables* (page 206)
1 egg, beaten
1 stick plus 1 tablespoon unsalted butter
⅔ cup granulated sugar
1 ⅓ cups blanched, sliced almonds
2 large whole eggs

To prepare the pears, combine the 2 cups of water and 1 cup of sugar in a wide saucepan and bring to a boil. Pare, core, and halve the pears and add them to the syrup. Boil gently until the pears are tender but slightly firm; the cooking time will vary from 2 to 5 minutes, depending on the ripeness of the fruit. A knife blade should meet some resistance when inserted into the pears. Remove pears from the syrup, cool and drain.

Grease the pie pan with the 1 tablespoon of butter.

Roll out the dough on a floured surface to a diameter of 12 inches and a thickness of ⅛ inch. Gently roll the dough around the rolling pin and unroll it onto the pie pan. Carefully, press down and form the dough against the pan. Trim the excess dough, leaving ¼ inch border of dough above the rim. Patch any tears with the dough trimmings. Chill the crust for ½ hour before baking. (Wrap and freeze the extra dough for later use.)

Preheat the oven to 375 degrees.

Prick the crust, bottom and sides with a fork. Cut a piece of wax paper to fit into the pie pan. Fill with rice, dried beans, or dough weights. In place of these, you may put a second pie pan bottom over the wax paper, thereby sandwiching the dough (see procedure on page 166). Bake for 6–8 minutes, remove from the oven and lift the dough weights and wax paper off of the crust. Brush the egg over the entire crust and bake for 10 more minutes until golden brown. While the crust is baking, prepare the custard.

To prepare the custard, place the almonds and ⅓ cup of sugar in a food processor, fitted with a steel blade. Grind the almonds to a meal for approximately 1 minute and set aside (overprocessing will result in an almond butter).

Soften the stick of butter and combine the remaining ⅓ cup of sugar. Cream together with an electric mixer on medium speed for about 1 minute. Add the flour and blend well. With the mixer still running, add the eggs one at a time, until each is incorporated. Pour in the almond meal, blending thoroughly.

To assemble the tart, pour the mixture into the pre-baked and slightly cooled pie crust (approximately ⅔ full). Place the pear halves, stem-end pointing center, in concentric circles, filling the pie shell. Return the tart to the 375 degree oven and bake for 25 more minutes, until the custard is set and nicely browned. Trim any excessively dark crust edges.

Serve at room temperature.

Monsieur François's hint to the home cook: try this pie using apricot or peach halves.

Tarte au Citron Vert

Lime Tart

Serves 6 to 8

1 9-inch pie shell (page 166)
3 limes
1 stick lightly salted butter
2 whole eggs
3 egg yolks
½ cup sugar
¼ cup whipping cream

Prebake a 9-inch pie shell.

While the pie shell is baking, finely grate the rinds of the limes and press to obtain the juice.

Melt the butter in a small saucepan. Remove from heat and mix in the grated rind and lime juice.

Using an electric mixer on high speed, whip the eggs and yolks with the sugar until the mixture whitens, approximately 5 minutes.

Add the cream and continue beating for 1 minute.

Pour the butter, rind, and juice into the egg and sugar mixture and blend a few seconds longer.

Fill the pie shell and bake in a 375-degree oven until the custard is set and lightly brown, about 20 minutes.

Allow the tart to cool before serving. Garnish with whipped cream.

Monsieur François's hint to the home cook: Try a lemon or orange tart using the same procedure.

Tarte aux Myrtilles

Blueberry Tart

Serves 6 to 8

1 9-inch pie shell (page 166), baked
1 pint fresh blueberries, with stems removed
2 tablespoons kirsch
3 tablespoons butter
¼ teaspoon finely grated lemon rind
2 egg yolks
2 whole eggs
½ cup sugar
1 cup heavy cream
¼ teaspoon vanilla extract

Wash the blueberries and drain well.

Place the cleaned blueberries in a small bowl and add the kirsch. Mix with a spoon and allow to marinate while preparing the rest of the ingredients.

Preheat oven to 375 degrees.

Melt the butter in a small saucepan. Remove from heat and add the lemon rind.

Combine the yolks, whole eggs, and sugar in a deep bowl. Beat well with an electric mixer on high speed until the mixture whitens, approximately 5 minutes. Turn mixer down to low; pour in the heavy cream, vanilla, and lemon butter. Beat for 10 seconds.

Place the blueberries and kirsch in the baked pie shell. Pour the custard over the berries and bake in the oven for 30 to 35 minutes, until custard sets and is lightly browned on top.

Let the pie cool before serving.

Monsieur François's hint to the home cook: This recipe is also excellent with huckleberries.

Tarte aux Framboises

Raspberry Tart

Serves 6

1 strip puff pastry (page 167), 16 by 5 by ⅛ inches
2 strips puff pastry, 16 by ¾ by ⅛ inches each
1 egg beaten with 1 tablespoon cold water
1 tablespoon *framboise* (raspberry brandy)
¾ cup pastry cream (page 168)
1 pint raspberries

Meringue:
6 egg whites
Pinch of salt
⅔ cup sugar
½ teaspoon finely grated lemon rind
¼ teaspoon vanilla extract
Pastry bag with medium star tube

Place the large strip of puff pastry on an ungreased baking sheet. With a small pastry brush, coat a 1-inch border lengthwise on both sides of the pastry strip with the egg. Press the two narrow strips of pastry over the egg coating. Using the tines of a fork, thoroughly prick the bottom layer of the pastry, but not the side strips. (You want those to rise.)

Bake in a 375-degree oven for 15 minutes, or until golden brown. Remove from oven and cool.

Beat the *framboise* into the pastry cream with a whisk.

Increase the oven temperature to 425 degrees.

With the baked puff pastry still on the baking sheet, fill the center with the pastry cream. Cover the cream with the raspberries, reserving six.

To prepare the meringue, combine the egg whites and salt in a very clean bowl. Whip with an electric mixer on medium speed, slowly adding the sugar as the meringue forms. Add the lemon rind and vanilla, whipping until soft peaks form. Do not overwhip!

Fill the pastry bag with the meringue and pipe over the berries in a decorative pattern. The berries must be completely covered. Immediately place in the hot oven. Bake until golden brown, approximately 5 minutes. Turn the pastry after about two mintues, as the back of the oven is warmer than the front.

Remove, cool for several minutes, and decorate by placing the six reserved raspberries in a line down the center of the pastry.

Monsieur François's hint to the home cook: Serve within one hour.

Tarte au Fromage

Sour Cream Cheese Cake

This cake is, of course, as American as apple pie. However, using a French name heightens the expectation.

Serves 8 to 10

Graham cracker crust:
1 ¼ cup graham cracker crumbs
⅓ cup brown sugar
¼ teaspoon cinnamon
¼ teaspoon nutmeg
⅓ cup melted unsalted butter

Filling:
2 whole eggs
¾ cup sugar
2 teaspoon vanilla extract
¼ teaspoon grated lemon rind
1 ½ cup sour cream
1 pound soft cream cheese
2 teaspoons melted butter

Place graham cracker crumbs in a mixing bowl. Add sugar, spices, and melted butter, and stir until crumbs are moistened.

Press mixture thinly and evenly into a buttered 5-cup spring mold.

Put eggs, sugar, vanilla, lemon rind, and sour cream in a food processor; cover and blend on high speed for 15 seconds. With motor on, gradually add the soft cream cheese and 2 teaspoons melted butter.

Pour mixture into the prepared pan and bake in a preheated 375-degree oven for 30 to 40 minutes, or until set in center. Overcooking will cause large cracks. The filling will still be slightly soft but will firm as the cake cools.

Chill thoroughly and garnish with seasonal fruits before slicing.

Monsieur François's hint to the home cook: The ovens at L'Auberge are calibrated once a month. Many home ovens are wildly off the mark and the cooking times indicated may vary.

Crème Renversée au Caramel

Caramelized Custard

Serves 10

Molds:
10 4-ounce ramekins
1⅓ cups sugar
½ cup water

Custard:
4 cups milk
⅔ cup sugar
grated rind of ½ lemon plus ½ orange
1 tablespoon vanilla extract

To prepare the molds, combine the sugar and water in a small saucepan. Place over high heat and boil to a light brown caramel, shaking the pan occasionally. Immediately, pour a little of the caramel into the 10 ramekins, lifting each to coat the bottoms evenly. Set aside.

Preheat the oven to 350 degrees.

To prepare the custard, combine the milk, sugar, and the lemon and orange rinds in a saucepan. Place over high heat to scald, i.e. boil the milk. Remove from heat and stir in the vanilla extract. Allow to cool for a few minutes.

With a wire whisk, beat the eggs in a stainless steel or glass bowl. Slowly, pour the warm milk into the eggs, whisking constantly. (Pouring the milk too rapidly will cause the eggs to curdle.)

Set the molds in a roasting pan that is approximately 10 by 20 by 2½ inches. Pour hot water into the roasting pan, so that the water comes halfway up the sides of the ramekins.

Bake for about 20 minutes, until the custards are set. Insert a small knife near the edge of one of the molds. If the blade comes out clean, the custards are sufficiently cooked.

Remove from the oven lift the ramekins out of the water bath, and chill completely before serving.

To serve, run a knife around the edge of each ramekin. Invert a small plate over the mold and turn over. Then lift the mold.

Mousse au Chocolat

Chocolate Mousse

Serves 10 (or 6 chocoholics)

1 stick unsalted butter
6 ounces dark bittersweet chocolate (see hint on page 170)
5 eggs yolks
2 tablespoons dark rum
2 cups heavy whipping cream
8 egg whites
Pinch of salt
⅔ cup sugar

Melt the butter and chocolate together over a low flame in a heavy saucepan. Stir often to avoid scorching. Remove from the heat and cool slightly.

Stir the egg yolks into the chocolate one at a time, blending thoroughly. Add the 2 tablespoons of rum and set aside.

Whip the cream in a chilled bowl.

Whip the egg whites with a pinch of salt, slowly adding the sugar as the egg whites rise. Beat until soft peaks form.

Fold the chocolate into the whipped cream. Then fold the egg whites into the chocolate and cream mixture.

Transfer the mousse into individual ramekins or long-stemmed glasses and refrigerate.

Garnish with whipped cream and chocolate shavings before serving.

Mousse aux Parfums d'Alsace

Raspberry Brandy Mousse

One of the chef's many duties is selecting and tasting ingredients not only to gauge their freshness and flavor, but also to assess their marriageability with the other components of a particular dish. Wine is absolutely essential in *la cuisine française* and, of course, any brandies or other spirits must likewise be carefully evaluated. Due to the complex character of fine *vins* and alcohols, several tastings are usually required. The proper balance between the bouquet of the spirit and the essence of the principal ingredient must be struck. Only through careful analysis and years of tasting can this be achieved.

A chef, therefore, must put aside any personal considerations, and whether he wishes or not, must imbibe. It isn't that shouting orders in the volcanic heat of the kitchen makes him thirsty; or even that he needs relief from the pressures of his job. No! It is his duty. It's tough being a chef.

This recipe is inspired by those aromatic, *eaux-de-vie* fruit brandies for which Alsace is famous.

Serves 8

7 large eggs, separated
1 cup sugar
1 ½ ounces *framboise* (raspberry brandy)
2 cups heavy whipping cream
½ pint ripe raspberries
Pinch of salt

Combine the egg yolks and sugar in a copper or stainless steel bowl. Beat over simmering water until thickened to the consistency of a hollandaise sauce, about 5 minutes.

Remove from heat and stir in the liqueur.

Whip the cream and reserve.

Reserve eight large raspberries and coarsely chop the rest. Do not purée. Fold the raspberries into the whipped cream.

Whip the egg whites with a pinch of salt until soft peaks form. Carefully fold the egg yolk-sugar mixture into the whipped cream. Then fold in the whites. Taste and add more *framboise* if desired. Chill the mousse and the eight ramekins or stemware pieces for 1 hour.

Pipe the mousse into the serving ware using a pastry bag fitted with a star tube. Refrigerate.

Garnish the mousse with the reserved raspberries before serving.

Monsieur François's hints to the home cook: As the mousse is quite delicate, plan to prepare and serve it the same day. Just about any liqueur and fruit may be used for this dessert, in almost any combination. Fruit and liqueur flavors may be mixed, as well as matched.

Gratin de Framboises

Glazed Raspberries

Serves 4

5 egg yolks
½ cup sugar
5 tablespoons *framboise* (raspberry brandy)
⅓ cup heavy whipping cream
1 pint fresh raspberries

Combine the yolks and sugar in a stainless steel or copper bowl. Place over simmering water and cook, beating constantly until the mixture thickens to the consistency of a hollandaise sauce. Remove from the heat and let the mixture cool completely.

Add 1 tablespoon of the *framboise* to the yolk mixture. Whip the cream and fold into the yolk mixture.

Preheat the broiler. Divide the raspberries into four shallow oven-proof dishes. Pour 1 tablespoon of the *framboise* over the fruit in each dish. Then coat the fruit completely with the sauce. (The sauce must cover the fruit completely or it will scorch.) Place the dishes under the broiler until the sauce is lightly brown, 1 to 2 minutes. Serve immediately.

Monsieur François's hint to the home cook: Use any seasonal fruit or a combination of fruits.

Gâteau au Chocolat

Chocolate Cake

Serves 16

1 recipe *biscuit de savoie* (chocolate sponge cake, page 169)
1 recipe *crème au beurre au chocolat* (chocolate butter cream,
   page 170)
1¼ cups toasted slivered almonds
¾ cup chocolate shavings

Sugar syrup:
½ cup sugar
1 cup water
1 tea bag
2 tablespoons dark rum

Boil the sugar and water. Remove from the heat, add the tea bag, and steep for 10 minutes. Cool the syrup and add the rum.

To assemble the cake, cut cake horizontally into thirds, using a serrated knife. Remove the two top thirds and set aside. Using a small pastry brush, coat the bottom section evenly with one-third of the syrup.

Spread a ½-inch thick layer of butter cream over the bottom. Set the second layer on top and repeat the two previous steps. Place the third layer on top, coat it with remaining syrup, and spread a thin layer of butter cream over the entire surface of the cake.

Press almonds around the sides of the cake.

Spoon the remaining butter cream into a pastry bag fitted with a small star tube and pipe butter cream in a decorative pattern around the edge of the cake.

Monsieur François's finishing touch: Garnish the top of the cake with chocolate curls (made by scraping a block of chocolate with the flat edge of a knife or potato peeler). Chill the cake before serving.

Gâteau aux Framboises

Raspberry Cake

Serves 16

3 cups heavy whipping cream
2 tablespoons powdered sugar
2 ½ tablespoons *framboise* (raspberry brandy)
1 recipe *biscuit de savoie* (chocolate sponge cake, page 169)
1 pint fresh raspberries (reserve 12 of the best for garnish)
1 cup chocolate shavings

Simple syrup:
½ cup sugar
1 cup water

Combine the sugar and water for the syrup in a heavy saucepan and bring to a full boil. Remove from the heat and cool completely. This can be prepared in advance and stored, covered, in the refrigerator.

Whip the heavy cream in a chilled bowl with the sugar.

Stir the *framboise* into the syrup.

Cut the cooled cake into three layers, horizontally.

Place one layer on a serving dish and cover evenly with one-third of the syrup, using a pastry brush. Cover with a layer of whipped cream, about ½ inch thick. Distribute half of the raspberries over the whipped cream, pressing them gently into the cream.

Place the second layer on top of the berries and repeat as above.

Brush the cut side of the third layer with the remaining syrup and flip over on top of the assembled cake.

Frost the cake, top and sides, with the remaining whipped cream. Sprinkle the top and sides with the chocolate shavings and arrange the 12 remaining raspberries around the edge.

Chill before serving.

Monsieur Francois's hint to the home cook: This recipe may also be prepared in the same manner using strawberries.

Vacherin Glacé au Kirsch

Ice Cream in Meringue Cups

This recipe was tested by Robert Shoffner, wine and food editor for the *Washingtonian* magazine.

Serves 8

10 egg whites
Pinch of salt
½ teaspoon vanilla extract
½ lemon rind, finely grated
1 cup sugar
1 pint whipping cream
Kirsch
Fresh strawberries for topping

Whip egg whites at high speed with a pinch of salt until the mixture begins to thicken. Add vanilla extract and lemon rind and continue whipping, while adding the sugar, 2 to 3 tablespoons at a time. Whip until the mixture stands up in stiff peaks.

Preheat oven to 300 degrees.

Spoon the mixture into a pastry bag fitted with a star tube. Form eight meringue nests on a Teflon or parchment lined cookie sheet. Bake in the oven for 25 minutes. Turn off the oven and leave the meringue nests there to dry for 1 to 2 hours. Store in an airtight container.

When ready to serve, fill the meringue nests with a scoop of vanilla ice cream, sprinkle each with a teaspoon of kirsch, top with freshly whipped cream, and decorate with strawberries.

Monsieur François's hint to the home cook: Garnish the *vacherin* with any seasonal fruit.

Mille-Feuilles aux Fruits Frais

Fresh Fruit Napoleon

Serves 6

3 strips puff pastry (page 167), 16 by 5 by ⅛ inches
2 tablespoons Grand Marnier (orange liqueur)
2 cups pastry cream (page 168)
¾ cup heavy whipping cream
¼ teaspoon vanilla extract
1 tablespoon sugar
6 to 8 fresh strawberries
½ cup fresh raspberries
½ cup powdered sugar
1 kiwi fruit

Preheat oven to 400 degrees.

Place the strips of puff pastry on an ungreased baking sheet and prick all over with the tines of a fork. Bake for 12 to 15 minutes, or until golden brown. Remove from the oven and cool. These strips may be baked ahead of time. However, do not assemble the napoleon more than 1 hour before serving.

In a small bowl, blend the Grand Marnier into the pastry cream. Whip the heavy cream with the vanilla extract and sugar until firm. Store in the refrigerator.

To assemble the napoleon, place 1 sheet of the puff pastry on a serving dish and spread with half the pastry cream. Then slice the strawberries and spread them evenly over the pastry cream. Be sure that each serving has some fruit on it.

Place the second sheet of pastry on top of the first and cover with the remaining pastry cream.

Place the raspberries on top of the cream and top with the last sheet of pastry. Dust the top generously with the powdered sugar.

Place a clean metal poker or a wide barbecue skewer over direct heat until it is red hot. Put the poker on the pastry only an instant to caramelize the sugar. Mark the surface in a criss-cross grid pattern.

Spread the whipped cream on all four sides of the pastry with a spatula.

Peel and slice the kiwi fruit and arrange it down the center of the pastry.

Refrigerate and serve within the hour.

Monsieur François's hint to the home cook: Use whatever seasonal fruits are available in the napoleon.

Soufflé glacé aux Fraises

Frozen Strawberry Soufflé

Serves 8

1¾ cups strawberry purée, made from approximately 1 pound
    whole berries
½ cup water
1 cup sugar
6 egg whites
Pinch of salt
1½ cups heavy whipping cream
4 tablespoons *fraises* (strawberry brandy) or kirsch
8 whole strawberries
Butter

Coulis de fraises (strawberry sauce):
2 cups strawberry purée, made from approximately 1¼ pounds
    whole berries
¾ cup sugar
2 tablespoons kirsch

Wash all the strawberries for both the soufflé and the sauce in cold water. Be sure to lift the berries out of the water, leaving the grit behind. Cap the berries and purée in a food processor. Measure 1¾ cups of purée and set aside.

To make the sauce, mix ¾ cup sugar and 2 tablespoons kirsch with the remaining 2 cups of purée. Refrigerate until time to serve.

To make the soufflé, prepare an Italian meringue by combining the water and sugar in a heavy saucepan and boiling until the mixture reaches 280 degrees, or the soft crack stage on a candy thermometer. When the thermometer reaches 250 degrees, begin whipping the egg whites and the pinch of salt in an electric mixer. Whip until soft peaks form. When the sugar reaches 280 degrees, remove the pan from the heat. With the electric mixer on low, slowly pour the boiled sugar into the whites. Continue whipping for 4 to 5 minutes to cool the meringue.

Whip the heavy cream in a chilled bowl.

Stir the 4 tablespoons of brandy into the 1¾ cups of reserved strawberry purée. Fold the purée into the cooled meringue. Then gently fold the whipped cream into the strawberry-meringue mixture. Chill while preparing the soufflé molds.

To assemble the soufflé, butter eight 4-ounce ramekins and eight 12-by-3-inch strips of parchment paper or aluminum foil. The foil must stand 1 inch above the rim of the molds. Form a collar around each mold with a strip of foil, buttered side facing in, and secure with tape.

Fill each mold to the very top of the collar with the meringue mixture and freeze several hours. Before serving, remove the collar and top each soufflé with one of the strawberries. Serve with the sauce on the side.

Monsieur François's hint to the home cook: The soufflés may be prepared with almost any fruit.

Charlotte glacée aux Framboises

Frozen Raspberry Charlotte

Makes 16 individual charlottes

1 ¾ cups raspberry purée, approximately 1 ½ pints
½ cup water
1 cup sugar
6 egg whites
Pinch of salt
1 ½ cups heavy whipping cream
6 tablespoons *framboise* (raspberry brandy)
32 lady fingers
1 cup sugar syrup (page 185)
Butter

Coulis de framboises (raspberry sauce):
3 cups raspberry purée, approximately 2 pints
1 ¼ cups sugar
4 tablespoons *framboise* (raspberry brandy)

Purée all 3 ½ pints of raspberries in a food processor or blender. Strain through a fine sieve to remove the seeds; 4 ¾ cups of purée should remain. Measure 1 ¾ cups of purée and refrigerate.

To make the sauce, mix 1 ¼ cups of sugar and 4 tablespoons of framboise with the remaining 3 cups of purée. Chill until time to serve.

To prepare the charlottes, make an Italian meringue by boiling the water and sugar until the mixture reaches 280 degrees or the soft crack stage on a candy thermometer. When the temperature reaches 250 degrees, begin whipping the egg whites and the pinch of salt with an electric mixer. Continue beating until soft peaks form. When the soft crack stage is reached, remove the pan from the heat and with the mixer on low speed, slowly pour the boiled sugar into the whites. Continue whipping for 4 to 5 minutes to cool the meringue.

Whip the heavy cream in a chilled bowl. Stir 4 tablespoons of *framboise* into the 1 ¾ cups reserved raspberry purée and fold into the Italian meringue. Then gently fold the whipped cream into the raspberry meringue mixture. Refrigerate while preparing the charlotte molds.

To assemble the charlotte, butter sixteen 4-ounce ramekins. Cut the 32 ladyfingers in half. Stir in remaining 2 tablespoons of *framboise* into the cup of sugar syrup. Dip the ladyfinger halves into the syrup for an instant. Place one in the bottom, and three equally spaced around the inside of each ramekin.

Fill the prepared molds with the charlotte mixture and freeze at least 2 hours prior to serving. The charlottes may be prepared a day ahead.

To serve, run a knife around the inside of the molds. Dip the molds in hot water for 2 to 3 seconds; then invert into the center of a serving dish to unmold. Pour the sauce around the charlottes and serve.

Monsieur François's hint to the home cook: Prepare the charlottes with strawberries, black currants, blackberries or other fruit.

Toasted Almond Butter Cream Charlotte

Papa arrived at L'Hotel Chambard ready to begin learning *la grande cuisine*. However, his first job as an apprentice was to clean all the windows in the hotel. As time passed, window washing and potato peeling were assigned to newer apprentices, and Papa moved up to actual cooking and baking. The first dessert he learned to prepare at the hotel was this almond charlotte, the house specialty.

Serves 12

Crème anglaise (**custard**):
3 cups milk
Grated rind of ½ orange and ½ lemon
10 egg yolks
1¾ cups sugar

Mold:
½ cup sugar
½ cup water
½ ounce kirsch
½ stick unsalted butter
16 ladyfingers, split
1 12-cup loaf pan (5½ by 5 by 11 inches)

Charlotte:
3¼ cups whole almonds, shelled but not peeled
1¼ pounds unsalted butter
1 ounce kirsch

To prepare the custard, combine the milk, orange and lemon rind. Scald the milk in a 2-quart copper or stainless steel saucepan.

Beat the egg yolks and sugar together with an electric mixer on high speed until the mixture turns white and forms a ribbon. Reduce speed and slowly pour the scalded milk into the yolk mixture.

Return the ingredients to the saucepan and cook slowly over low heat, stirring constantly with a wooden spoon or rubber spatula. Heat until the custard coats the spoon, but do not boil. Immediately remove the saucepan from the heat. Stir occasionally while the sauce is cooling, and then refrigerate.

To prepare the mold, boil the sugar and water. Allow to cool and stir in the kirsch.

Thoroughly butter all sides and bottom of the mold.

Dip each ladyfinger half into the cooled syrup for an instant and line the bottom first, then the sides of the mold. Eight ladyfingers should remain to cover the top. Chill.

191

To prepare the charlotte, spread the almonds on a baking sheet and toast in a 400-degree preheated oven until light brown, approximately 10 minutes. Cool (discarding any that are excessively dark as they are bitter) and grind in a food processor to the consistency of coarse meal. Set aside.

Cut the butter into small pieces, put in a large mixing bowl, and allow to soften but not melt.

Butter and *crème anglaise* should be approximately room temperature.

Add the kirsch to the *crème anglaise*. Using a wire whisk, whip the butter a few moments and slowly pour in the *crème anglaise*, whipping constantly. When all the *crème* is emulsified in the butter, mix in the ground almonds and immediately pour into the mold. Top the mixture with the remaining ladyfingers. Cover with a foil or plastic wrap and refrigerate at least 2 hours before serving.

Unmold the charlotte and slice with a hot knife. Garnish with whipped cream and fresh fruit.

Monsieur François's finishing touch: Serve the charlotte with *coulis de framboise* (raspberry purée, page 190), if desired.

Terrine de Chocolat glacé,
Sauce Praline

Chocolate Terrine with Praline Sauce

Serves 16 to 20

Praline:

1 cup shelled hazelnuts,
   approximately ⅓ lb.
½ cup sugar
4 tablespoons water

Custard Sauce

2 cups milk
4 egg yolks
½ cup sugar
¼ cup heavy whipping cream
2 tablespoons Frangelico (hazelnut liqueur)

Molds:

4 tablespoons butter
32 3-inch ladyfingers, split
2 collapsible loaf pans,
   (13 by 4 by 9 inches)

Mousse:

3 egg whites
pinch of salt
¾ cup granulated sugar
½ cup water
1 cup heavy whipping cream
½ stick unsalted butter
8 ounces bittersweet chocolate
   (see hint on page 170)
1 ounce dark rum

To prepare the molds, line bottoms and sides of pans with ladyfinger halves. Refrigerate.

   To prepare the mousse, make an Italian meringue by combining the water and sugar in a saucepan and boiling until the mixture reaches 280 degrees or the soft crack stage on a candy thermometer. When the temperature reaches 250 degrees, begin whipping the egg whites and the pinch of salt with an electric mixer. Whip until soft peaks form. When the sugar reaches 280 degrees, remove from the heat and with the mixer on low, slowly pour the boiled sugar into the whites. Continue whipping for 2 to 3 minutes to cool the meringue.

   Combine the ½ stick of butter and the eight ounces of chocolate in a small heavy saucepan. Melt over low heat, stirring frequently. When throughly blended, remove from the heat. Stir in the rum and set aside to cool.

Whip the heavy cream and refrigerate.

Fold the cooled chocolate and butter mixture into the Italian meringue. Then gently fold in the whipped cream. Taste and add more rum if desired.

Fill the prepared molds with the chocolate mousse and cover with the remaining ladyfinger halves. Cover with foil or plastic wrap and freeze at least four hours before serving.

To prepare the praline, preheat the oven to 400 degrees. Spread the hazelnuts in one layer on a sheet pan and toast in the oven until the skins blister and darken, approximately 8 to 10 minutes. Immediately wrap the nuts in a towel and rub vigorously to remove the skins. (Not all the skins will come off, but this will not affect the outcome of the recipe.) Wipe clean and lightly oil the tray used to roast the hazelnuts.

Combine the sugar and water in a medium saucepan and cook over a high heat to a light brown caramel, about 4 to 5 minutes. Add the nuts and mix thoroughly with a spoon to coat all the hazelnuts. Pour the mixture onto the sheet tray and allow to cool at least 15 minutes.

Break the mass of nuts and sugar into small pieces with the dull side of a cleaver. Place in a food processor, fitted with a steel blade. Add 1 teaspoon vegetable oil and grind to a coarse paste (about 3 to 4 minutes).

To prepare the custard, scald the milk in a heavy saucepan and remove from the heat.

Beat the eggs, yolks and sugar together in a stainless steel bowl until the mixture whitens. Slowly pour the milk into the yolks while beating constantly. Transfer the custard to a heavy stainless steel saucepan or double boiler and cook over moderately high heat, stirring constantly, until it coats a spoon. Remove from the heat and immediately stir in the heavy cream. Strain the custard through a fine sieve into a bowl and thoroughly blend in a hazelnut paste. Add the Frangelico. Chill in refrigerator until ready to serve.

To serve, unmold the terrines and cut each into 8 to 10 slices with a serrated knife. Place each slice on a chilled plate and pour 2–3 tablespoons of praline sauce around each. Garnish with whipped cream and chopped hazelnuts or almonds.

Monsieur François's hint to the home cook: Line the molds with slices of sponge cake, rather than ladyfingers. Mix blanched chopped hazelnuts into the mousse before freezing.

Kugelhopf en neige Vanillé

Soft Baked Meringue with Vanilla Sauce

This recipe was home-tested and edited by Marian Burros, author of *Pure and Simple*. Becoming exasperated when my initial recipe failed to work, she requested and received a demonstration right in the restaurant's kitchen.

Serves 10

⅓ cup golden raisins
2 tablespoons kirsch
½ teaspoon unflavored gelatin
2 tablespoons water
12 egg whites
2 tablespoons grated orange rind
2 tablespoons grated lemon rind
1 teaspoon vanilla extract
1 ¼ cups sugar
3 kiwi fruit
Kugelhopf sauce (page 197)

Caramel glaze:
½ cup sugar
½ cup water

Combine raisins and kirsch in a cup. Let macerate overnight at room temperature to absorb the flavor.

Sprinkle the gelatin over the water in a small saucepan; stir to mix. Let stand 5 minutes to soften. Heat over a very low flame, stirring constantly, just until the mixture clears and the gelatin is dissolved.

Preheat oven to 300 degrees.

In a large bowl, combine the egg whites, orange and lemon rinds, dissolved gelatin, vanilla, and ½ teaspoon of the kirsch from the raisins. Beat with an electric mixer at high speed, just until foamy white. Add the sugar a few tablespoons at a time and continue beating until the meringue mixture forms stiff glossy peaks. Do not overbeat. Drain off any remaining kirsch from the raisins; fold the raisins into the meringue.

Spoon the mixture into a buttered and sugared 8-cup kugelhopf (a fluted tube pan) or 10-inch bundt pan. Cut through the mixture with a spatula to break up any large air bubbles; smooth the top. Place the pan in a larger deep pan and put the two pans on the bottom shelf of the oven. Pull the shelf out a little; pour boiling water into the outer pan so that it comes 3 to 4 inches up the side of the tube pan.

Bake in a slow oven for 30 minutes. Put a piece of foil over the top of the pan to keep the dessert from browning too fast. Bake 30 minutes longer, or until a cake tester inserted in the center comes out clean.

Remove the pan from the water to a wire rack. Run a knife around the edge and center tube to loosen. This will keep the dessert from tearing as it cools and shrinks slightly. Cool completely in a pan. While the cake cools, make the caramel glaze.

To serve, run a knife around the edge again; turn out on a serving plate. Spoon the caramel glaze over the meringue, making sure it covers the entire surface. Refrigerate until thoroughly cold, about 2 hours. Garnish with the sliced kiwi fruit, if you wish. Cut into serving pieces by bringing a knife blade down on the caramel glaze with quick chopping stroke, then slicing through the meringue. Surround each slice with kugelhopf sauce.

To prepare the caramel glaze, combine the ½ cup of sugar with the ½ cup of water in a small saucepan. Cook, shaking the pan occasionally, until the sugar melts and caramelizes to a golden brown. Watch carefully, as the difference between golden brown and burned glaze is a matter of seconds. The caramel will continue to cook in the pan even after it has been removed from the heat.

Crème Anglaise

Kugelhopf Sauce

Enough for one kugelhopf

¼ cup raisins
2 tablespoons kirsch
2 cups milk
8 medium egg yolks
¾ cup granulated sugar
¼ cup heavy whipping cream
¼ teaspoon vanilla

Begin the day before, by combining the raisins with the kirsch in a small bowl. Cover and soak overnight.

To prepare the sauce, scald the milk in a 2-quart copper or stainless steel saucepan.

Using an electric mixer or wire whisk, beat the yolks together with the sugar in a deep bowl until they turn white and form a ribbon. Continue beating, while slowly pouring the milk into the yolk mixture.

Transfer the ingredients back into the saucepan and cook slowly over a low flame, stirring constantly with a wooden spoon or a spatula. Heat until the custard coats the spatula, but do not boil. Immediately remove the saucepan from the heat and add the heavy cream to stop the cooking. Add the vanilla.

Transfer to a bowl and allow to cool. Before serving, add the raisins to the sauce. More kirsch may be added to taste.

Place a slice of kugelhopf on a plate and surround it with the sauce. Garnish with slices of kiwi or other fresh fruit.

Monsieur François's hint to the home cook: If the mixture separates, whipping at high speed will reconstitute the sauce.

Soufflé au Chocolat

Chocolate Soufflé
Individual Chocolate Soufflés

Serves 6

Double recipe of pastry cream (see page 168)
½ recipe of *crème anglaise* (see page 197)
7 ounces bittersweet chocolate (see hint on page 170)
6 egg yolks
⅓ cup milk
16 egg whites
2 ounces Cognac
6 teaspoons confectionery sugar
6 1½-cup ramekins
2 tablespoons unsalted butter
¼ cup granulated sugar

Prepare and thoroughly chill the pastry cream and *crème anglaise,* reserving the egg whites.

Preheat the oven to 400 degrees.

Butter and sugar the ramekins.

Combine the milk and chocolate in a heavy saucepan and place over low heat. Whisk the chocolate until completely melted and smooth (do not boil). Set aside.

Place the pastry cream in a large bowl and thoroughly whisk in the egg yolks. Pour the tepid chocolate into the pastry cream and blend well.

Place the 16 egg whites (4 from the *crème anglaise*, 6 from the pastry cream, and 6 from the soufflé recipe) and a pinch of salt in a mixing bowl. Beat at high speed until soft peaks form.

Combine ⅓ of the egg whites into the chocolate mixture with a rubber spatula. Lightly fold the chocolate pastry cream into the remaining beaten egg whites. Fill the prepared ramekins almost to the rim, being careful none of the mixture spills over the sides. Set the ramekins on a baking sheet and bake for approximately 25 minutes, until the soufflés are well risen.

While the soufflés are baking, mix the 2 tablespoons of cognac and the *crème anglaise*.

When the soufflés are cooked, remove them from the oven, dust with the powdered sugar, and serve at once.

Monsieur François's hint to the home cook: Timing is everything when making a soufflé. Your guests must await the soufflés, as they must go directly from oven to table.

After presenting the soufflé at the table, break open the top of each with a spoon and pour in a little sauce.

198

Glace à la Vanille

Homemade Vanilla Ice Cream

When my father was an apprentice, ice cream was prepared only on Sundays, owing to the lack of modern freezers. He had to shave the ice, mix it with the proper amount of salt, and then hand crank the mix until the correct consistency was reached. Today a number of excellent ice cream freezers are available for home use.

Makes 1½ quarts

2 cups milk
1 vanilla bean split, or 1 tablespoon pure vanilla extract
6 medium egg yolks
1 cup sugar
2 cups heavy whipping cream

Combine the milk and the split vanilla bean. Scald the milk in a heavy copper or stainless steel saucepan.

Beat the egg yolks and sugar together in a stainless steel bowl until the mixture whitens.

Slowly pour the hot milk into the yolks, beating constantly. Transfer the mixture back to the saucepan. Cook over simmering water or very low direct heat until the custard thickens and coats a spoon, but do not boil. Immediately pour in the heavy cream. (If you are using vanilla extract, it should be added at this point.)

Strain the custard into a bowl, cool, and refrigerate.

Freeze the custard according to directions for your machine. The ice cream is ready when it loses its sheen. Place in a covered freezer container and harden before serving.

Monsieur François's hint to the home cook: Despite the many high-quality sherbets and ice creams now commercially available, none equal those freshly made right in your own home. At L'Auberge, we make all our own frozen desserts. The following is a sampling of our most popular recipes. The ice creams will retain their flavors for at least one week. The sherbets, however, should be made and served the same day.

Glace au Chocolat

Chocolate Ice Cream

Makes 1½ quarts

2 cups milk
6 egg yolks
1 cup sugar
2 cups heavy whipping cream
5 ounces dark bittersweet chocolate (see hint on page 170)
⅓ cup chocolate chips

Scald the milk in a heavy copper or stainless steel saucepan.

Beat the yolks together with the sugar in a bowl, until they turn white and form a ribbon. Continue beating while slowly pouring the milk into the yolks.

Transfer the ingredients back into the saucepan. Cook over simmering water or a very low flame, stirring constantly with a rubber spatula. Heat until the custard coats the spatula, but do not boil. Immediately remove the saucepan from the heat and mix in 1 cup of the heavy cream.

Heat the 5 ounces chocolate with the remaining heavy cream in a small saucepan, until the chocolate has completely melted. Beat into the custard. Transfer to a bowl and allow to cool before refrigerating.

Freeze the custard according to the directions on your machine. When the ice cream is nearly set, add the chocolate chips. Place in a covered container and harden before serving.

Glace à la Praline

Praline Ice Cream

Makes 1½ quarts

Praline:
1½ cups shelled hazelnuts, approximately ½ lb.
⅔ cup sugar
2–3 tablespoons vegetable oil
¼ cup water

Ice Cream:
2 cups milk
6 egg yolks
⅔ cup sugar
2 cups heavy whipping cream

Preheat the oven to 400 degrees.

To prepare the praline, spread the hazelnuts in one layer on a sheet pan and toast in the oven until the skins blister and darken, about 8 to 10 minutes. Immediately, wrap the nuts in a towel and rub vigorously to remove the skins. (Not all the skins will come off, but this will not affect the outcome of the recipe.) Wipe clean and lightly oil the tray used to roast the hazelnuts.

Combine the sugar and water in a medium saucepan and cook over high heat to a light brown caramel, about 4 to 5 minutes. Add the nuts and mix thoroughly with a spoon, to coat all the hazelnuts. Pour the mixture on to the sheet tray and allow to cool at least 15 minutes.

Break the mass of nuts and sugar into small pieces with the dull side of a cleaver. Place in a food processor, fitted with a steel blade. Add 1 teaspoon vegetable oil and grind to a coarse paste (about 3 to 4 minutes).

To prepare the custard, scald the milk in a heavy saucepan and remove from the heat.

Beat the eggs, yolks, and sugar together in a stainless steel bowl until the mixture whitens. Slowly pour the milk into yolks while beating constantly. Transfer the custard to a heavy stainless steel saucepan or double boiler and cook over moderately high heat, stirring constantly, until it coats a spoon. Remove from the heat and immediately stir in the heavy cream. Strain the custard through a fine sieve into a bowl and thoroughly blend in hazelnut paste. Chill in the refrigerator before freezing.

Freeze the custard according to the instructions for your ice cream freezer.

Serve topped with whole hazelnuts.

Sorbet à la menthe

Mint Sherbet

Makes ½ quart

2 cups water
5 mint tea bags, or 1 cup fresh mint leaves
½ cup sugar
1 tablespoon finely minced fresh mint leaves
Several whole fresh mint leaves

Boil the water, remove from the heat, add the mint tea bags or the 1 cup of fresh mint leaves, and steep for 15 minutes.

Strain the mint tea, add the sugar to the warm liquid, and stir until completely dissolved. Cool and add the tablespoon of minced mint leaves.

Freeze according to the direction for the ice cream freezer, approximately 20 to 25 minutes. Cover and store in the freezer.

Serve in chilled glasses and decorate with whole mint leaves.

Sorbet au Cidre

Cider Sherbet

Makes ½ quart

2 cups fresh apple cider
½ cup sugar
1 tablespoon Calvados

Combine the cider with the sugar and stir until the sugar is dissolved. Freeze according to the directions for your ice cream freezer. Add the Calvados just at the end of the freezing cycle.

Remove from the freezer 5 to 10 minutes before serving.

Monsieur François's hint to the home cook: The sherbets will not set if less than the given amount of sugar is used.

Sorbet à l'Orange

Orange Sherbet

Makes ½ quart

¼ teaspoon grated orange rind (see hint below)
2 cups orange juice (approximately 6 oranges)
⅔ cups sugar

Stir the sugar into the orange juice and rind until completely dissolved. Freeze in an ice cream freezer and store, covered, in the freezer compartment. Remove from the freezer and let stand for 5 to 10 minutes before serving.

Monsieur François's hints to the home cook: Grate only the outermost rind of the oranges, as the white inner skin is very bitter.

Tangerine sherbet, one of my favorites, is made using the same formula as orange sherbet.

Sorbet au Citron

Lemon Sherbet

Makes ½ quart

¼ teaspoon grated lemon rind
1 cup lemon juice
1 cup water
¾ cup sugar

Grate only the outermost layer of rind, pressing lightly to avoid the bitter, white, inner skin.

Press the lemons to obtain 1 cup of juice. (Heating the lemons for 2 to 3 minutes in very hot water will greatly increase the yield.) Mix the juice and water. Add rind.

Stir the sugar into the lemon juice and rind until the sugar is completely dissolved.

Freeze according to the directions for your ice cream freezer. Cover and store in the freezer.

Remove 5 to 10 minutes before serving.

Monsieur François's hint to the home cook: The citrus fruit sherbets are especially suited for serving between courses to cleanse the palate.

Sorbet au Melon

Cantaloupe Sherbet

Makes ½ quart

1 large melon (or enough for 2 cups purée)
⅔ cup sugar
Juice of ½ lemon
Pinch of salt

Cut the melon in half and discard the seeds. Scoop out the flesh. Place in a food processor with the sugar, lemon juice, and salt, and purée the mixture.

Freeze according to the directions on your ice cream machine. Cover and store in the freezer.

Monsieur François's hint to the home cook: Any melon such as honeydew or Crenshaw may be used for this recipe. Slightly overripe melons are the best for making sherbets.

Sorbet à la Fraise

Strawberry Sherbet

Makes ½ quart

¼ pound whole strawberries (or enough for 2 cups purée)
¾ cup sugar
Juice of ½ lemon

Remove the stems and place the strawberries in a bowl of cold water; lift them out, leaving the dirt behind. Drain well.

Purée the strawberries in a food processor. Blend in the sugar and lemon juice.

Pour the mixture into an ice cream machine and freeze according to the manufacturer's instructions. The sherbet should stiffen in about 20 to 25 minutes. Cover and place in the freezer.

Remove the sherbet from the freezer about 10 minutes before serving.

Monsieur Francois's hint to the home cook: You may purchase frozen strawberries and prepare this sherbet year round.

Sorbet au Pamplemousse

Grapefruit Sherbet

Makes ½ quart

2 cups grapefruit juice (approximately 3 large grapefruits)
1 ⅓ cups sugar

Stir the sugar into the grapefruit juice until completely dissolved.
    Freeze according to the directions for your ice cream freezer. Let the sherbet stand at room temperature for 10 minutes before serving.

    Monsieur François's hint to the home cook: Do not strain the pulp out of the juice.

Sorbet aux Framboises

Raspberry Sherbet

Makes ½ quart

2 pints ripe red raspberries
1 cup of sugar

    Remove any stems from the berries and purée in a food processor. Force the purée through a fine sieve, to obtain 2 cups of seedless purée.
    Whisk the sugar into the purée.
    Freeze according to the directions on your ice cream machine. The sherbet should stiffen in approximately 20 minutes. Cover and freeze.

    Monsier Francois's hint to the home cook: Use the same method for black raspberries or blackberries.

Les Sablés

Sugar Cookies

Makes 180 2–3 inch cookies

½ pound unsalted butter
1 cup sugar
Pinch of salt
1 teaspoon vanilla extract
8 egg yolks
1 pound flour, sifted (about 3½ cups)
1 whole egg, beaten

Place the butter in a mixing bowl and soften at room temperature. Add the sugar, salt, and vanilla and cream thoroughly with an electric mixer. Add the egg yolks two at a time and blend well after each addition. Turn mixer to low speed and slowly add the flour.

Wrap dough in plastic and refrigerate 2 to 3 hours before baking.

Remove dough from refrigerator ½ hour before baking.

Preheat oven to 325 degrees.

Roll out the dough on a well-floured surface to a thickness of ⅛ inch. Cut into circles, or use any shape desired. Place on an ungreased baking sheet. Using a small pastry brush, coat each cookie with the beaten egg.

Bake for 10 to 12 minutes, or until lightly browned. Cool completely.

The cookies will keep several days if tightly covered.

Serve with ice cream or sherbet.

Monsieur François's hint to the home cook: Use this recipe to make Christmas cookies.

Le Vin Chaud

Hot Spiced Wine
A warming winter aperitif or evening drink before the hearth

While visiting my father's home town of Obernai, I stopped to place an order with the local vintner, Alphonse Seilly, whose wines are featured at L'Auberge. I facetiously asked if the wines he sent us were the same as those sold in Alsace. "Mon Dieu! mais oui!" he exclaimed. He pulled out a dozen bottles and glasses that I might verify the authenticity of his exported wines. Theoretically, to appreciate several wines one tastes without swallowing. However, I find this a great waste and always drink up. My recollection is admittedly somewhat hazy, but I do remember M. Seilly's wines tasted every bit as good as those served at L'Auberge.

Serves 12

Rind of 1 orange
Rind of 1 lemon
1 cup water
2 bay leaves
6 cloves
3 cinnamon sticks
1 cup sugar
1 gallon full-bodied red wine
½ cup honey
1 ounce cognac
Pinch of nutmeg

Remove the rind from the orange and lemon with a potato peeler.

In a 1 ½-gallon saucepan, combine the water, lemon and orange rind, bay leaves, cloves, cinnamon sticks, and sugar. Bring to a boil, reduce heat, and simmer for 15 minutes.

Add the wine and steep over low flame for 15 more minutes. The wine must not boil.

Remove from heat and stir in the honey, cognac, and pinch of nutmeg.

Strain the wine into a warm serving pitcher or bowl and serve.

Garnish each glass with a lemon and orange slice.

INDEX

Butter
  brown, skatefish in, 61
  clarified, 49
  cream
  —charlotte, toasted almond, 191-192
  —chocolate, 170
  garlic, 82
  herb, baked oysters in, 31
  sauces
  —anchovy, 55
  —for poached trout, 58
  —white, 51

Cabbage, braised
  red, 154
  white, 155
  —roast pheasant with, 121
Cailles aux raisin et baies de genièvre,
      124
Cailles farcies à notre façon, 125
Cakes. *See* Pastries and desserts
Canard, fonds de, 46
Canard aux pommes, sauce de, 48
Caneton du Long Island Bigarade, 116
Cantaloupe sherbert, 204
Capers, vinaigrette with onions, gherkins
      and, 54
Caramel glaze, 195,196
Caramelized custard, 181
Carrot(s)
  glazed, onions and, 150
  purée, 145
Cauliflower
  polonaise, 153
  purée, 146
  soup, 8
Céleriac rave remoulade, 141
Celery root
  julienne, rockfish with, 69
  salad, 141
Cervelle de veau au beurre noir, 109
Cervelle de veau sautée, 110
Champignons, crème de, 3
Champignons *à blanc,* 160
Chanterelles
  in puff pastry, sautéed, 27
  sautées, 151
  sweetbreads with, sautéed, 103
Charlotte
  raspberry, frozen, 190
  toasted almond butter cream, 191-92
Chartreuse de choux, 155
Châteaubriand with vegetables, 95
Cheese
  bacon and ham tarts, 15
  cake, sour cream, 180

salad, Swiss, 139
  spread, cottage, 14
Chestnut(s)
  cooking, 120
  peeling, 147
  purée, 147
  stuffing, 120
  —goose with, 118-19
Chicken
  in Alsatian Riesling wine, 114-15
  stock, 115
Chimney for pastry, 25, 26
Chocolate
  butter cream, 170
  cake, 185
  —sponge, 169
  ice cream, 200
  mousse, 182
  soufflé, 198
  Terrine with Praline Sauce, 193-94
Choucroute de poissons fumés, 75
Choucroute garnie Alsacienne, 98-99
Chou-fleur Polonaise, 153
Chou rouge braisé, 154
Choux-fleurs au gratin, purée, 146
Christmas cookies, 206
Cider sherbet, 202
Civet de marcassin, 132-33
Clam chowder, Boston, 5
Concombres, salade de, 139
Cookies, sugar, 206
Coq au Riesling d'Alsace, 114
Coquillages. See Shellfish
Corn Salad and Belgian Endive, 137
Cotes de Veau Farcies Strasbourgeoise,
      104-5
Cottage cheese spread, 14
Coulis de fraises (strawberry sauce), 189
Coulis de framboises (raspberry sauce),
      190
Courgettes Niçoise, 156
Court Bouillon (aromatic broth), 36
Crabmeat
  artichokes stuffed with, cold, 33
  broiled lobster stuffed with, 83
  melon stuffed with, 90
  mousseline of crayfish and, 84-85
  in puff pastry, 28
Crabs, soft-shell, with almonds, 79
Cranberry sauce, 56
Crayfish
  mousseline of crab and, 84-85
  sauce, 84
Cream and mushroom sauce, 96
Creamed soups. *See* Soups
Crécy, purée, 145

217